To Cecilia
With best wi...
Good luck with your classes.
Ben Wetz

ADVENTURES

Student's Book

Pre-Intermediate

Ben Wetz

OXFORD
UNIVERSITY PRESS

Unit and Topic	Grammar	Vocabulary
1 **Personality** page 5	• Present simple • Present continuous • Present simple and present continuous	• Personality: adjectives • Adverbs of manner
2 **Crime** page 13	• Past simple • Past continuous • Past simple and past continuous • Subject and object questions	• Crimes • Verbs from crime stories
The World of English 1 page 21	• Revision: present simple, present continuous, past simple, past continuous	• Everyday language
3 **Tasty!** page 27	• Pronouns: *some ...* , *any ...* and *every ...* • Countable and uncountable nouns • *a lot of*, *many* and *much* • *(not) enough*, *too much* and *too many*	• Food • Preparing food: verbs and adjectives
4 **Buy and sell** page 35	• Comparative and superlative adjectives • *going to* and *will* • *too* and *(not) ... enough*	• Shopping • Adjectives
The World of English 2 page 43	• Revision: *going to*, *will*, *(not) ... enough*, comparatives	• Everyday language
5 **Work** page 49	• Present perfect • Present perfect: *ever* and *never* • Present perfect: *yet* and *already*	• Jobs • Adjectives: qualities for jobs
6 **Extreme** page 57	• Present perfect and past simple • Present perfect: *for* and *since* • Present perfect: *just*	• Sports • Sports equipment
The World of English 3 page 65	• Revision: present perfect	• Everyday language
7 **Microchip magic** page 71	• *will* and *might* • First conditional • Second conditional	• Computers • Movement: verbs + prepositions • The internet
8 **Rules** page 79	• *can*, *could*, and *be allowed to* • *have to* and *must*	• Legal and illegal • Household tasks and objects
The World of English 4 page 87	• Revision: first conditional, second conditional, *have to*, *must*	• Everyday language
9 **Money** page 93	• The passive: present simple • The passive: past simple	• Money • Production and consumption
10 **News and views** page 101	• Past perfect • Reported speech	• News topics • Fame: adjectives and nouns
The World of English 5 page 109	• Revision: reported speech, past passive, modal verbs	• Everyday language

Grammar pages 115–123   Vocabulary pages 124–128   Irregular verbs inside back cover

Reading and Listening	Speaking	Writing	Pronunciation and Study skills
• Handwriting • Body language • Chalk and Cheese	• Describing personality • Asking about how people do things	• Describing people: using modifiers	• Word stress • Reading tips
• Crazy criminals • Confess • Murder Mystery	• Doing a questionnaire • Talking about a crime	• A confession: *so* and *because*	• /ə/ and weak forms (1)
• North Street: Episode 1 • Culture File • Story of Pop: Rock and roll	• Making arrangements: *Are you doing anything … ? How about … ing? OK. Let's …*	• Project: planning a short talk	• Rhythm and intonation
• Hard Rock Café • Food, fat and fibre • Strange tastes	• Talking about likes and dislikes • Asking about restaurants	• Cooking instructions: *first, then, after that* and *finally*	• Silent vowels
• In the supermarket • Shopping • Adverts	• Asking about shops, products and adverts • Discussing a present	• Using comparisons • Planning an advert	• Intonation
• North Street: Episode 2 • Culture File • Story of Pop: Soul	• Shopping: *Can I help you? I'm looking for … I'll have that one, thanks.*	• Project: making a poster or leaflet	• Rhythm and intonation
• Dream jobs • The ladder of success • Interviews	• Asking about experiences • Playing a board game • Asking about careers • Asking interview questions	• A formal letter	• /h/ • Guessing the meaning of words from context
• The summit • Skysurfers • Risk	• Asking about sports • Discussing risky situations	• Presenting factual information	• Recognizing contractions
• North Street: Episode 3 • Culture File • Story of Pop: Merseybeat	• Making suggestions: *Why don't you …? You should definitely …*	• Project: writing about problems	• Rhythm and intonation
• Game over • Virtual world • Websites	• Spelling computer vocabulary • Giving opinions about the future • Discussing the future	• Organizing ideas: mind maps • Describing a website	• The alphabet: revision
• Banned! • Strict or soft? • Rules	• Giving opinions about what should be legal or illegal • Discussing rules • Asking about jobs at home	• Expressing contrast: *however, although, but* and *on the other hand* • Planning school rules	• /ə/ and weak forms (2) • Agreeing rules in class
• North Street: Episode 4 • Culture File • Story of Pop: Ska and reggae	• Giving opinions: *I think that … Don't you agree? No, I don't agree with you. Why's that? Well, because …*	• Project: making a poster	• Rhythm and intonation
• Making money • The story of money • Teenage millionaires	• Talking about money • Doing a role play	• An autobiography: organizing a paragraph	• /j/ • Improving your communication skills
• True stories • Exclusive! • Good news	• Explaining past events • Roleplaying an interview • Asking about an event	• A news story: summary sentences	• /-ed/
• North Street: Episode 5 • Culture File • Story of Pop: Disco	• Making offers and requests: *Could you … ? I'll …*	• Project: making a poster	• Rhythm and intonation

OXFORD
UNIVERSITY PRESS

Great Clarendon Street, Oxford OX2 6DP

Oxford University Press is a department of the University of Oxford.
It furthers the University's objective of excellence in research, scholarship,
and education by publishing worldwide in

Oxford New York

Auckland Cape Town Dar es Salaam Hong Kong Karachi
Kuala Lumpur Madrid Melbourne Mexico City Nairobi
New Delhi Shanghai Taipei Toronto

With offices in

Argentina Austria Brazil Chile Czech Republic France Greece
Guatemala Hungary Italy Japan Poland Portugal Singapore
South Korea Switzerland Thailand Turkey Ukraine Vietnam

OXFORD and OXFORD ENGLISH are registered trade marks of
Oxford University Press in the UK and in certain other countries

© Oxford University Press 2003

The moral rights of the author have been asserted

Database right Oxford University Press (maker)

First published 2003

2008 2007 2006

10 9 8 7 6

No unauthorized photocopying

All rights reserved. No part of this publication may be reproduced,
stored in a retrieval system, or transmitted, in any form or by any means,
without the prior permission in writing of Oxford University Press,
or as expressly permitted by law, or under terms agreed with the appropriate
reprographics rights organization. Enquiries concerning reproduction
outside the scope of the above should be sent to the ELT Rights Department,
Oxford University Press, at the address above

You must not circulate this book in any other binding or cover
and you must impose this same condition on any acquirer

Any websites referred to in this publication are in the public domain and
their addresses are provided by Oxford University Press for information
only. Oxford University Press disclaims any responsibility for the content

ISBN-13: 978 0 19 437662 4
ISBN-10: 0 19 437662 1

Printed in China

ACKNOWLEDGEMENTS

The author would like to dedicate this book to Adam Black

The authors and publisher are grateful to those who have given permission to reproduce the following extracts and adaptations of copyright material: National Geographic.com homepage, p 82, reproduced courtesy of National Geographic Society

Blue suede shoes, p 95. Words and Music by Carl Perkins. © 1956 by Hi-Lo Music Inc. Public performance rights for USA and Canada controlled by Hi-Lo Music Inc., a BMI affiliate. All other rights in the world controlled by Unichappell Music Inc (Rightsong Music Publisher). All rights reserved. Lyrics reproduced by permission of Carlin Music Corp., London NW1 8BD

Nowhere to run, p 96. Words and Music by Brian Holland, Lamont Dozier and Eddie Holland. © 1965 Stone Agate Music/Jobet Music Co. Inc., USA. EMI Music Publishing Ltd, London WC2H 0EA. Reproduced by permission of IMP Ltd

Can't buy me love, p 97. Words and music by John Lennon and Paul McCartney. Reproduced by permission of Sony/ATV Music Publishing

I can see clearly now, p 98. Words and Music by Johnny Nash (c) 1986 Cayman Music Inc., Dovan Music Inc., Vanas Music Inc. and Vanas Music, Netherlands. Warner/Chappell Artemis Music Ltd, London W6 8BS. Reproduced by permission of International Music Publications Ltd. All Rights Reserved

We are family, p 99. Words and music by Bernard Edwards and Nile Rodgers. © 1979 Bernard's Other Music/Warner-Tamerlane Publishing Corp., USA. Reproduced by permission of IMP Ltd (50%) and Song/ATV Music Publishing (50%)

Illustrations by: Kathy Baxendale p 6 (handwriting); Michael Bury/Inkshed pp 14, 28; France Chaulet/Private View pp 23, 36, 45, 67, 89, 111; Jason Ford pp 17, 29, 42 (shop), 100 (Monopoly); Adam Graff p 31 (apples, breakfast), 33, 97, 108; Phil Hankinson pp 31 (shopping), 34, 42 (objects), 53 (Ken & Liz), 61, 64 (sports left), 80 (objects), 83 (shopping), 102; Mark Harrison pp 20 (thief), 53 (Himalayas), 59, 64 (sports right); Paul Howalt/Three-in-a-Box p 20 (verbs); Monica Laita/New Division pp 7, 9, 12, 37 (all), 39, 41, 56, 83 (household objects), 95; Pierre Paul Pariseau p 30; Andy Parker pp 16, 72, 73 (Castle Master), 78 (Castle Master); Mike Stones/Illustration pp 41 (Petal perfume), 52, 60; Dylan Teague pp 13, 18, 19; Lucy Truman pp 24, 25 (globe)

We would like to thank the following for permission to reproduce photographs: Action Plus p 63 (surfing); Alamy p 24 (airport); Allsport p 57 (canoeing, sailing); Ancient Art & Architecture p 96 (knife money); Apple Mac p 78 (keyboard, mouse); Bank of England p 94 (destroying notes); John Birdsall pp 43 (Indian family), 84 (girl, mother); Camera Press pp 98 (Harry Potter), 101 (room, politics, concert), 106 (cable car rescue/Scanpix); Camera Work/Michael Cole p 98 (Jennifer Capriati); Chard p 96 (Argentinian and Leonardo Da Vinci coin); Corbis pp 47 (San Gennaro, Chinatown), 87 (frisbee), 90 (frisbee), 113 (Thanksgiving story); Haddon Davies p 112 (Christmas); Environmental Picture Library/David Hoffman p 79 (protest); Eyewire p 86 (coffee machine), 96 (Kennedy coin); Fujifilm p 40 (airship); Gateway p 71 (computer, printer, scanner, mouse, speakers), 78 (monitor); Getty Images pp 10 (Ann), 25 (Hatsue/David Allan Brandt, Claudia/Mark Dolphin, Rob/ Frank Orel, Ivan/Fisher&Thatcher), 42 (check-out), 50 (snowboarder), 55 (both), 56 (snowboarder), 57 (parachuting, skateboarding), 59 (canoeing), 60 (skysurfing), 65 (girl in window), 68, 74 (internet), 85 (Reuben and Wayne), 86 (dishwasher, washing machine, David), 90 (yoyo), 93 (credit card, gold, vault), 101 (graph), 104, 114 (glittery boots, disco); Robert Harding pp 57 (snowboarding, surfing), 93 (bank); Hulton Getty pp 70 (Beatles left), 80 (slaves, suffragettes), 81 (Sultan Murad IV); Honda p 101 (robot); Hwadong p 96 (FIFA WC coin); Imageworks p 69 (metal detector); Ingram Publishing p 5 (frames 7 and 8); Katz Pictures pp 32 (woman eating insect, plate of crickets), 47 (Cotton Club), 50 (DJ), 51 (child worker), 74 (Benetton Billboard); The Kobal Collection pp 7 (werewolf), 79 (Amistad), 98 (Macauley Culkin); Naoto Kosako/Time Magazine p 29; London Features International pp 87 (Jimmy Cliff), 92 (Jimmy Cliff); Mary Evans Picture Library p 80 (prohibition, soldiers); Monnaie de Paris (kindly provided by Euro Collections Ltd) p 96 (Children's Euro); North News and Pictures Ltd p 84; Photodisc pp 5 (all frames except 7 and 8), 69 (surveillance camera, ID mugshot), 71 (joystick, webcamera), 99 (football), 78 (webcamera, joystick, Lucy), 86 (cooker), 90 (skateboard, pogo stick, skates), 106 (girl); Photofusion pp 35 (shelf/Ray Roberts, price/Corry-Bevington, special offer/Bob Watkins), 46, (mosque), 90 (skates, Pogo stick, skateboard); Popperfoto p 74 (wrist mobile); Powerstock/Zefa pp 10 (Sally), 79 (grafitti), 93 (cashpoint); Redferns pp 26 (dancing, Freed), 43 (Martha Reeves), 48 (all), 65 (Beatles), 70 (Beatles right), 92 (reggae); Helen Reilly pp 40 (Nike haircut); The Reserve Bank of Australia/Note Issue Department p 94 (making notes); Retna p 57 (diving), 109 (Sister Sledge); Rex Features pp 21(Elvis), 26 (Elvis), 40 (cows), 46 (Ganesh), 69 (sniffer dog), 70 (Beatlemania), 74 (MP3, computerized clothes), 101 (war), 112 (Thanksgiving), 114 (Sister Sledge); The Royal Canadian Mint/Image de la pièce courtoisie de la Monnaie royale canadienne p 96 (maple coin); Rubberball Productions/Getty Images p 90 (hula hoop); Science Photo Library pp 33 (chocolate scorpion); 34 (astronaut eating); 79 (pills), 101 (medicine/Mauro Fermariello, seabird/John Watney); Herb Swanson p 107 (crashed lorry); Thinkstock/Getty p 101 (graph); Sony p 73 (dog); Tropicana p 35 (slogan, logo); Trip/Art Directors pp 47 (Immigration Museum), 57 (skiing), 58, 69 (police patrol), 85 (Aki), 86 (iron, mop, Tessa); John Walmsley p 11; Rikio Watanabe p 96 (Egyptian coin)

Commissioned photography: Emily Andersen: Photostory + pp 8, 38 (shoe shop), 46 (Josie), 49

The World of English: pp 43, 45, 46, 87, 109

Steve Betts: pp 12, 27, 28, 37 (Harry Potter), 38 (shoes, boots), 54, 82, 93, 95, 113 (cards)

The World of English: pp 91, 109

1 Personality

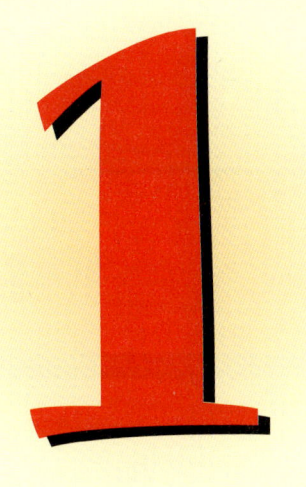

Have a look!
Find the pages where you:
- listen to a conversation about body language.
- write about a friend.
- read about handwriting analysis.

Vocabulary
Adjectives describing personality

1 Copy the adjectives in the box. Find pairs of opposites.

> active   confident   friendly   cheerful   lazy
> honest   quiet   dishonest   ~~aggressive~~
> moody   shy   ~~calm~~   unfriendly   talkative

aggressive – calm

2 In pairs, check your answers.

VOCABULARY PAGE 124, 1.1

3 Listen and repeat the words in exercise 1.

Speaking

4 Work in pairs. Describe and identify the people in the photos.

> A: *She's about 30 years old. I think that she's confident and friendly.*
> B: *Number 8?*
> A: *Yes.*

1a Handwriting

Reading

1 Read and listen. Is the analysis correct for your handwriting?

Graphology — writing and personality

Graphology is the study of handwriting. Experts say that handwriting tells us about people's personality. What does your handwriting say about you? Are you confident or shy? Lazy or active? Compare your handwriting with this analysis.

Angle

Left — *Your writing goes this way.*
You're shy. You go out with people, but you aren't very confident. You're sometimes moody, but you don't show your feelings.

Right — *Your writing goes this way.*
You've got a lot of energy. You're confident and you're very active. You usually act before you think. You like people and you show your emotions. You don't think before you speak.

Straight — *Your writing doesn't go left or right.*
You're a quiet person and you control your feelings. You think before you speak. You're interested in the present – you don't think much about the past or the future.

Mixed — *Your writing goes left and right.*
Your mood often changes. You're cheerful one moment and moody the next moment. Your friends don't always understand you.

Size

Small — *Your handwriting is small.*
You're quiet and you usually work alone. You watch people and you think about things a lot. You don't like big groups, but you aren't unfriendly.

Big — *Your handwriting is big.*
You're friendly and confident, but sometimes you're very talkative. You relax when you meet people. You've got a big personality and you like action!

2 Look at Jenny and Matt's handwriting. Are the sentences true or false?

Jenny: *Hi! My name's Jenny. I'm 16.*

Matt: *Hello. I'm Matt. I'm from Ottowa, in Canada.*

1 She doesn't show her emotions.
2 She doesn't think before she speaks.
3 She relaxes when she meets people.
4 He likes big groups.
5 He thinks a lot and controls his emotions.

Pronunciation

Word stress

3 Listen and repeat.

a ■	b ■□	c □■
1 likes	3 quiet	5 control
2 calm	4 people	6 compare

4 Add the words to columns a–c. Then listen and check.

1 relax *c*   3 active   5 doesn't
2 does   4 alone   6 thinks

Exploring grammar
Present simple

5 Look at exercise 2. Complete the table.

	Affirmative	Negative
I / you / we / they	think	don't think
he / she / it	(1)	(2) ......
Questions		
Do	I / you / we / they	think?
Does	he / she / it	think?

GRAMMAR PAGE 115

6 Complete the text. Use the present simple form of the verbs.

Wolfman Jack
Jack usually **works** (work) in an office. He's quiet. He (1) ...... (not go out) much at night. He (2) ...... (prefer) to stay at home. But sometimes his personality (3) ...... (change). He (4) ...... (become) an animal and he (5) ...... (go out) a lot. He (6) ...... (eat) out, but he (7) ...... (not go) to restaurants.

7 Complete the sentences. Use the present simple affirmative or negative forms of the verbs in the box.

laugh   go   play   do   ~~speak~~   study   listen

My mates
Ruth and Kate are quiet. They **don't speak** (speak) a lot. Ruth is patient — she always (1) ...... to people's problems. Ed is lazy — he (2) ...... at school and sometimes he (3) ...... his homework. Ed and Kate aren't very active. They (4) ...... sport. Ed and Mick are cheerful — they (5) ...... a lot. Mick is very friendly. He often (6) ...... out with people.

8 Put the words in order. Then answer the questions.

Do you control your emotions?
Yes, I do.

1 Do / relax / in big groups of people? / you
2 you / before you speak? / usually think / Do
3 Does / often change? / your mood
4 usually show / Do / you / your feelings?
5 think about things / Do / a lot? / you
6 Does / left or right? / your handwriting / go

Speaking

9 Work in pairs. Ask and answer the questions in exercise 8. Then think of more questions.

Finished?
Look at the handwriting of a friend in the class. Write sentences about his/her personality.

Unit 1 *Personality*

1b Body language

Listening

1 Look at the picture and listen to a conversation about body language. Match four names in the box with the people in the picture.

> Kerry   Mary   Deb   Sylvie   David   Martin

2 Complete the sentences about body language with the words in the box. Then listen again and check.

> honest   ~~defensive~~   happy
> comfortable   aggressive   dishonest

1 Sometimes when we cross our arms and legs it is a *defensive* gesture.
2 We often point a finger at a person when we're angry. This is …… .
3 We move away from a person when we aren't …… with them.
4 When we're …… to be with a person, we often mimic their gestures.
5 …… people make open gestures with the palms of their hands.
6 …… people sometimes avoid eye contact when they aren't telling the truth.

Exploring grammar
Present continuous

3 Look at the examples.

Affirmative
He's **pointing** his finger at her.
They're **sitting** over there.
Negative
She **isn't speaking** to him.
They **aren't telling** the truth.
Questions
What **are** you **reading**, John?

GRAMMAR ▶ PAGE 115

4 Write true and false sentences about the picture. Then read out your sentences.

Tom is smiling. (True)
John is standing near Alex. (False)

Present simple and present continuous

5 Complete the table with rules a and b.

Present simple	
(1)	People **make** gestures.
Present continuous	
(2)	Kerry **is looking** at a magazine. You**'re meeting** him tonight.

a We use this tense to talk about an action that is happening at the moment or future arrangements.

b We use this tense to talk about routines or repeated actions.

GRAMMAR PAGE 115

6 Complete the dialogue. Use the present simple or the present continuous.

Tim: Why *are* you *sitting* (sit) here alone?
Ann: I (1) ...... (not want) to talk.
Tim: But why the sad face? Is it Mark again? What (2) ...... he ...... (do) now?
Ann: He (3) ...... (talk) to Isabel.
Tim: But he often (4) ...... (talk) to people. He's friendly.
Ann: Look! Now they (5) ...... (dance).
Tim: Relax. Why (6) ...... you ...... (shout)?
Ann: Because he never (7) ...... (dance) with me!

Vocabulary

Adverbs of manner

7 Listen and choose the correct words.
1 They're laughing **loudly** / **quietly**.
2 He's walking **quickly** / **slowly**.
3 They're singing **happily** / **sadly**.
4 She's speaking **calmly** / **angrily**.
5 She's playing **well** / **badly**.

8 Look at exercise 7. Make a list of adjectives and adverbs of manner. How do we form most adverbs of manner?

Adjective	Adverb
loud	loudly
quiet	

VOCABULARY PAGE 124, 1.2

9 Write questions. Use the present simple and adverbs of manner.

Do you smile happily in photos?

1 ... speak English (good)?
2 ... sing (bad)?
3 ... eat (slow)?
4 ... talk about problems (calm)?
5 ... spend money (intelligent)?
6 ... play sport (aggressive)?
7 ... laugh (loud)?

Speaking

10 Work in pairs. Ask and answer the questions from exercise 9.

Do you smile happily in photos?
Yes, usually.

Finished?

Write sentences about people you know. Use the adverbs in exercise 9.
My sister plays the guitar well.

Unit 1 *Personality*

1c Chalk and cheese

Speaking

1 **Work in groups. Discuss the question.**

What is the biggest influence on your personality?

- your family
- your friends
- your experiences
- where you live
- television
- the weather

Reading

2 **Guess which sentence is true: 1, 2 or 3. Then read and listen and check your answer.**

1 Only genes influence your personality.
2 Parents and friends don't influence your personality.
3 A lot of things influence your personality.

Chalk and Cheese

1 Sally and Ann are sisters. They're both quite tall and they've got dark hair and brown eyes. Physically they're very similar, but their characters are different. Sally's really
5 confident. She's always talking and joking, and she does things quickly. Ann isn't very energetic. She's more serious and she does things calmly and slowly. She's happiest when she's sitting quietly reading a book.

10 'They're like chalk and cheese,' says Alice, their mother. 'I think Sally and I are similar. We're both quite loud and extrovert. But Ann has got her father's character – she's a bit shy and she doesn't go out a lot.'

15 Sally and Ann are different because they've got a different mix of genes. Genes influence our physical appearance and our personality. Perhaps you've got your mother's eyes and your grandfather's terrible temperament. Or perhaps
20 you've got your father's nose and your grandmother's fantastic character!

Experts say that about 50 per cent of our personality comes from our genes. The other 50 per cent of our personality depends on our
25 experiences. Many different things influence us: our home life, our school, our friends and the TV, for example. All of us have different lives, and all of us have different personalities.

Sally Bushell, 17

Ann Bushell, 16

Study skills
Reading tips

3 Look at the advice about reading. Complete the sentences with the words in the box.

> general ~~first~~ every some

1 The *first* time you read a text, read it quickly and try to understand the …… meaning.
2 When reading for detail, it's a good idea to check the meaning of …… words in a dictionary.
3 It isn't necessary to check the meaning of …… new word.

4 Find words 1–8 in the text in exercise 2. Complete the table.

1 physically   4 extrovert   7 temperament
2 characters   5 per cent   8 experience
3 chalk   6 mix

I need to check the meaning.	I don't need to check the meaning.
physically	*characters*

5 Read the text again and answer the questions.

1 Are Sally and Ann very different physically?
2 Describe Ann's character.
3 Is Sally and Ann's father extrovert?
4 How much of our personality depends on our genes?
5 Do our experiences influence our personality?

Writing
Describing people: using modifiers

6 Look at the text again. Complete the notes with *a bit, not very, quite, very* and *really*.

1 Ann and Sally – physically …… similar
2 Sally – …… confident
3 Ann – …… energetic
4 Sally and her mother – …… loud
5 Ann and her father – …… shy

7 Complete the text with the words in the box.

> a bit   really cheerful   really talkative
> ~~really good~~   very different
> not very moody

John's a *really good* friend. We met 8 years ago at primary school. We don't go to the same school now, but he lives near me and I often see him. John's the same age as me and we've got the same interests. But our personalities are (1) ……. I'm quite quiet, but he's (2) ……. The best thing about John is that he's (3) …… and he always jokes about things. He's (4) …… or unfriendly. Sometimes he's (5) …… bossy, but when he's like that I don't listen to him.

8 Write about a friend. Include this information:

- Where did you meet this person?
- How often do you see this person?
- How are you similar?
- How are you different?
- Why do you like this person?
- What's the best thing about this person?

Finished?

Write sentences about you and your family. Use modifiers.

I'm similar to my mother. We're both quite quiet.

Progress Check 1

Adjectives describing personality

1 Put the letters in order. Then write the opposites of the adjectives.

docfentin – *confident – shy*

1 fluecher
2 lefyrind
3 tequi
4 azyl
5 stohen
6 grassvigee

Adverbs of manner

2 Match 1–6 with a–f to form adjectives. Then write the adverbs of manner.

angry – angrily

1 an
2 ca
3 lo
4 hap
5 go
6 qui

a et
b py
c od
d gry
e ud
f lm

Present simple

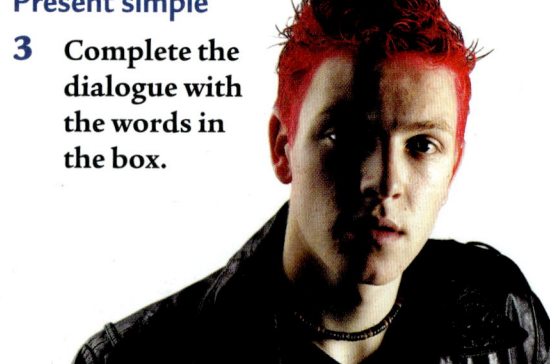

3 Complete the dialogue with the words in the box.

does ~~Does~~ don't change don't doesn't do does changes

Jan: *Does* your personality influence your appearance?
Lee: Yes, it (1) …… . My appearance (2) …… .
Jan: Why does it (3) …… ?
Lee: I (4) …… want to be boring.
Jan: What (5) …… your parents think?
Lee: Mum's OK, but dad (6) …… like my hair.
Jan: What (7) …… he say about your hair?
Lee: Not much. We (8) …… speak about it.

Present continuous

4 Put the words in order. Then answer the questions.

Where are you sitting?
I'm sitting in the classroom.

1 What / you / are / doing?
2 you / working hard? / Are
3 sitting / Who / behind you? / is
4 the teacher / is / wearing? / What
5 Is / speaking loudly? / the teacher
6 meeting friends / you / Are / on Saturday?

Present simple and present continuous

5 Complete the sentences with the correct form of the verbs. Use the present simple and the present continuous.

1 Ella and Tom …… (go) to school at the moment.
2 School …… (start) at 8.45 a.m.
3 Ella …… (smile) at Tom.
4 Tom …… (not look) at Ella.
5 Tom usually …… (walk) to school.
6 He …… (play) football after school with some friends.

12

2 Crime

Have a look!
Find the pages where you:
- write a confession.
- read some true crime stories.
- listen to detectives interviewing a man.

Vocabulary

Crimes

1 Match some of the words in the box with crimes 1–6.

> kidnapping   murder   robbery
> pickpocketing   ~~smuggling~~   vandalism
> drug dealing   speeding

1 smuggling

2 Listen and repeat the words in exercise 1.

3 Decide which crimes are the most serious. Make a list.

1 murder

VOCABULARY PAGE 124, 2.1

2a Crazy criminals

Reading

1 Read and listen. Then match stories 1–4 with pictures a–d.

Crazy criminals –
true stories from the mad, sad world of crime

1. When murderer Daniel Mitchem escaped from prison in New Mexico, USA, he went to his house and hid. At first the police didn't find him in the house, but they looked for him in the fridge when Mitchem's young daughter said, 'Daddy's in there!' Mitchem was very cold when the police arrested him.

2. Police in Sweden stopped a woman at an airport because they suspected her of smuggling. The woman had 65 baby snakes in her clothes. When the police asked her about the snakes, the woman confessed. 'I wanted to start a snake farm,' she said.

3. A robber in Brazil planned to steal some music equipment from a social club. First he stole a car and then he went to the club. He found the music equipment, but he also found a lot of food. He ate some chicken and some ice cream, and then he drank 30 glasses of beer. What did the police discover when they went to the club the next morning? The robber asleep on the floor!

4. Two armed robbers tried to steal money from a shop in New York City, but they didn't succeed. One of the robbers shot his partner by accident, and they started to argue. The police soon arrived and they arrested both men.

2 Read stories 1–4 and answer the questions.
1. Where was Daniel Mitchem before he went to his house?
2. How was he when the police found him?
3. What did the smuggler want to do with the snakes?
4. What did the Brazilian robber do before he went to the club?
5. What did he do in the club?
6. Why didn't the robbers steal any money from the shop in New York?

Vocabulary

Crime stories: verbs

3 Read stories 1–4 again and find verbs 1–9. Then write the infinitives of the verbs and guess the meanings.

escaped – escape

1. hid
2. arrested
3. suspected
4. confessed
5. planned
6. stole
7. found
8. discovered
9. shot

VOCABULARY PAGE 124, 2.2

14

Exploring grammar
Past simple

4 Read stories 1–4 again and find these things.

1. The past simple forms of **escape**, **look**, **stop** and **try**.
2. The past simple forms of **go**, **be**, **have** and **hide**.
3. Two negative sentences in the past simple.
4. One question in the past simple.

5 Look at your answers to exercise 4. Are the sentences true or false?

1. Irregular verbs end in -ed in the past simple.
2. We make negative sentences in the past simple with *didn't*.
3. We make questions in the past simple with *do*.
4. The past simple describes a finished action in the past.

GRAMMAR ➤ PAGE 116

6 Complete the stories with the correct form of the verbs in the boxes.

> complain   succeed   ~~try~~

More crazy crimes
Two men *tried* to escape from prison, but they didn't (1) ...... because another prisoner (2) ...... about the noise.

> try   find   listen

In Italy a hypnotist (3) ...... two robbers in his office. He (4) ...... to hypnotize the men, but they didn't (5) ...... to him.

> go   take   not find

A robber in Kansas (6) ...... into a café to steal some money. When he (7) ...... any money, he locked the manager in the kitchen, served the customers and (8) ...... their money.

7 Complete the questions with the words in the box.

> Did   did   ~~become~~   did   How   do

When did you *become* a criminal?
1. Where ...... you commit your last crime?
2. What did you ...... when the police found you?
3. ...... did you feel when the police arrested you?
4. How long ...... you stay in prison?
5. ...... your life change after prison?

Subject and object questions

8 Read story 1 in exercise 1 again. Then match the questions with answers.

1. Who found Daniel Mitchem?
2. Who did the police find?
a. **The police** found him. (subject)
b. They found **Daniel Mitchem**. (object)

GRAMMAR ➤ PAGE 116

9 Read stories 2, 3 and 4 in exercise 1 again. Complete the questions.

(have / the smuggler) What *did the smuggler have* in her clothes? Snakes.
1. (stop / the smuggler) Who ...... at the airport? The police.
2. (find / the robber) What ...... in the club? Music equipment and a lot of food.
3. (drink / 30 glasses of beer) Who ......? The robber.
4. (shoot / one of the robbers) Who ...... in the shop? His partner.
5. (do / the police) What ...... when they arrived? They arrested the robbers.

Finished?
Imagine that you are a 'crazy criminal'. Write answers to the questions in exercise 7.
I became a criminal five years ago.

2b Confess!

Listening

1 Read the police document and listen. Do the detectives think that Terry is innocent?

```
Interview with:   Terry Adams
          Date:   Tuesday 18th February
          Time:   10.05
Officers present: Detective Inspector Fry
                  and Detective Constable Smith

DC Smith: Are you Terry Adams of 14 Pearce Street?
   Adams: Yes, I am.
DC Smith: Did you know that there was a robbery last night, Terry?
   Adams: A robbery? No! Where?
   DI Fry: OK, Terry. What exactly were you doing last night at
           eleven o'clock?
   Adams: I was watching DVDs at home.
DC Smith: Ha, ha! Very funny.
```

2 Listen to the rest of the interview. Match times from the box with pictures 1–3.

> 10.45   11.00   11.15   11.30   12.00

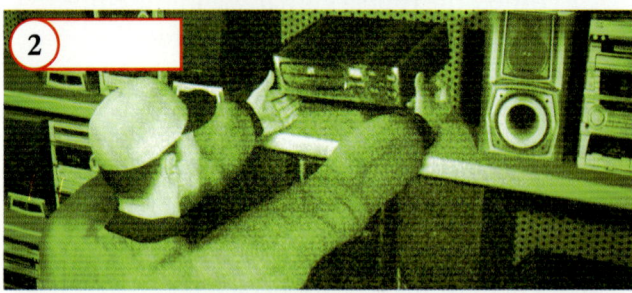

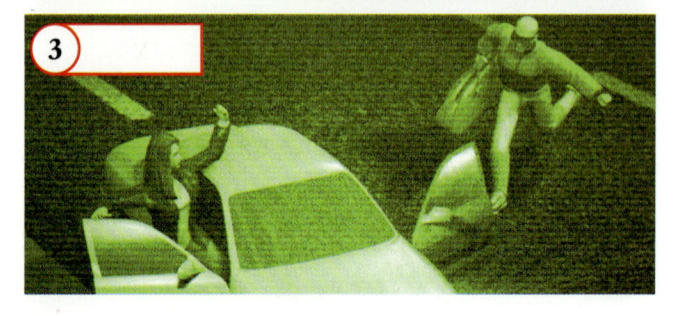

3 Listen again and answer the questions.

1 Can Terry remember the name of the film?
2 How many DVD players did he steal?
3 What does Terry think of the man on the police video?
4 What sport does Terry like?
5 Where were Carol and Jim waiting?

Exploring grammar

Past continuous

4 Complete the table with *was*, *were* and *wasn't*.

Affirmative	
I / He / She / It	was running.
You / We / They	(1) ...... waiting.
Negative	
I / He / She / It	(2) ...... running.
You / We / They	weren't waiting.
Questions	
Where (3)	Terry standing?
What (4)	you doing?

GRAMMAR PAGE 117

5 Complete the dialogue. Use the past continuous of the verbs.

A: What *were* the guards *doing* (do) when prisoner 23 escaped?

B: They (1) …… (talk). They (2) …… (not watch) the prisoners.

A: (3) …… the other prisoners …… (work)?

B: One prisoner (4) …… (work). The others (5) …… (play) cards.

A: And what (6) …… the dog …… (do)?

B: It (7) …… (sleep).

6 Complete the detective's questions. Then invent answers. Use the past continuous.

1 What / you / do / at two o'clock this morning?
2 Why / you / carry / a TV?
3 Why / you / wear / gloves and dark clothes?
4 your friend / work / with you?
5 Why / your friend / sit / in a car?

Past simple and past continuous

7 Complete the rules with 'past simple' or 'past continuous'.

The *past continuous* describes an action in progress in the past.
He **was running** down the street.
The (1) …… describes a finished action in the past.
I **saw** him.
We can use the past simple and the past continuous together. This is the 'interrupted past'.
He **was running** down the street when I **saw** him.
The (2) …… describes the longer action. The (3) …… describes the shorter action or interruption.

8 Complete the sentences with the correct form of the past simple and past continuous.

Questionnaire: are you a good citizen?

1 You …… (walk) on a beach yesterday when you …… (find) some diamonds in a plastic bag. What did you do?

2 The police …… (stop) you last week because you …… (ride) a motorbike without a helmet. What did you do?

3 You …… (see) two criminals this morning. They …… (steal) from a car. What did you do?

4 People …… (sell) illegal copies of CDs in the street and your friend …… (buy) one. What did you do?

5 You …… (talk) to your 13-year-old neighbour yesterday and she …… (start) to smoke. What did you do?

6 You …… (break) an egg when you …… (shop) in a supermarket. What did you do?

Pronunciation

/ə/ and weak forms 1

9 Listen and repeat. Is the /ə/ sound stressed or unstressed?

1 You w<u>e</u>re walking down th<u>e</u> street.
2 He w<u>as</u> sitting in <u>a</u> car.

10 Practise saying the sentences. Then listen and repeat.

1 It w<u>as</u> <u>a</u> robbery. Th<u>e</u> p<u>o</u>lice w<u>e</u>re there.
2 W<u>ere</u> th<u>e</u> robb<u>e</u>rs in <u>a</u> car?

Speaking

11 Work in pairs. Imagine the situations in exercise 8. Ask and answer the questions. Is your partner a good citizen?

Finished?
Write more questions for the questionnaire.

Unit 2 *Crime*

2c Murder mystery

Listening

1 Look at the newspaper report and the notes. Answer the questions.
   1 How did Ivor Bundell die?
   2 Where were the clues?
   3 How many suspects are there?

May 6th

Mystery of millionaire's murder

Millionaire businessman Ivor Bundell is dead. He died after a party at his Hollywood home. There was poison in his coffee. Detectives are now investigating the crime.

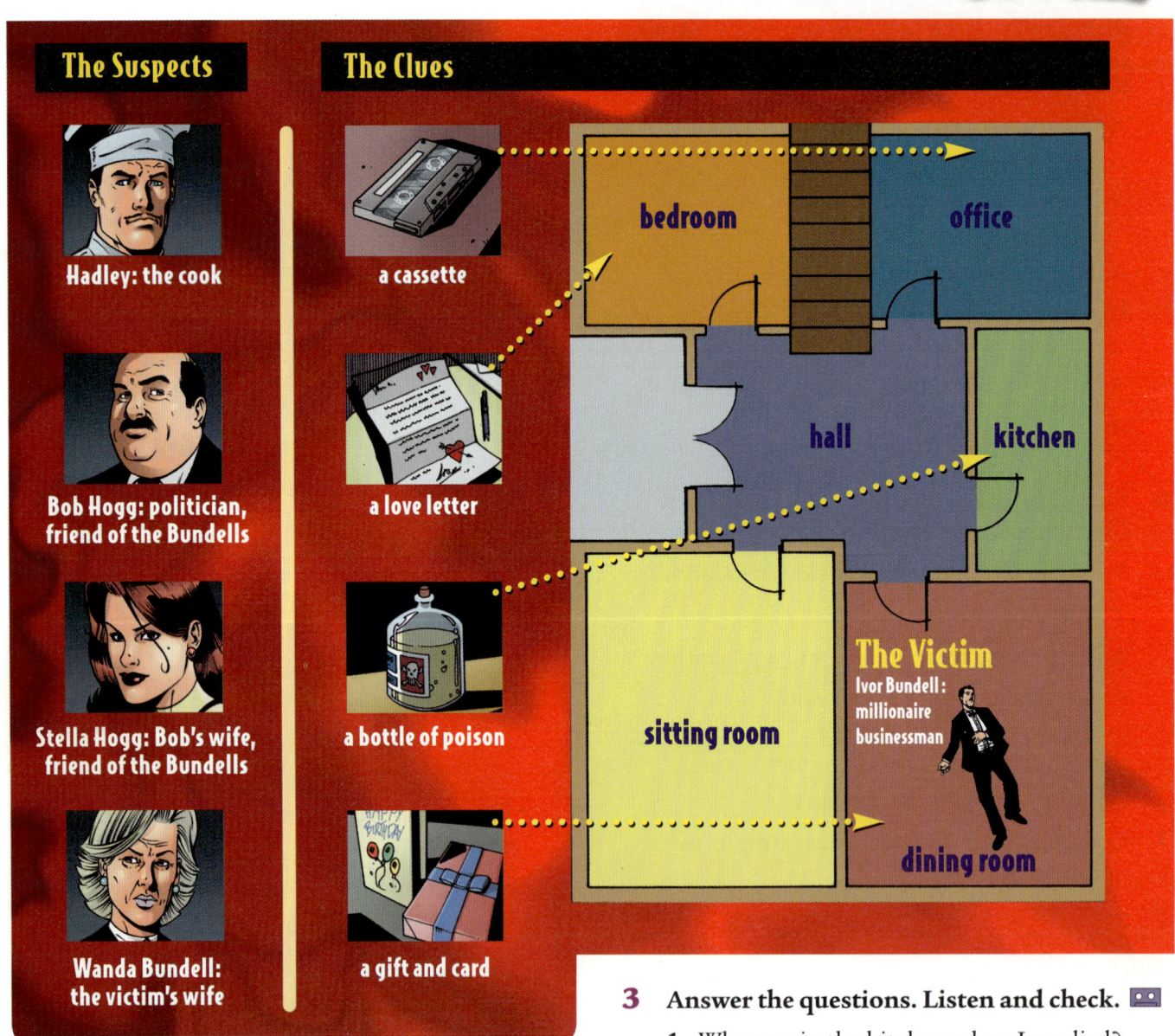

The Suspects

- Hadley: the cook
- Bob Hogg: politician, friend of the Bundells
- Stella Hogg: Bob's wife, friend of the Bundells
- Wanda Bundell: the victim's wife

The Clues

- a cassette → bedroom
- a love letter → bedroom
- a bottle of poison → kitchen
- a gift and card → dining room

Rooms: bedroom, office, hall, kitchen, sitting room, dining room

The Victim
Ivor Bundell: millionaire businessman

2 A detective is interviewing the suspects. Listen to the conversation. Who <u>doesn't</u> speak to the detective?
   1 Hadley
   2 Bob Hogg
   3 Stella Hogg
   4 Wanda Bundell

3 Answer the questions. Listen and check.
   1 Who was in the kitchen when Ivor died?
   2 Who was talking to Ivor before he died?
   3 Who wanted to borrow money from Ivor?
   4 Who recorded a conversation?
   5 Why did Stella give a present to Ivor?
   6 Who did Stella accuse?

Speaking

4 Who murdered Ivor? Read Stella's opinion. Do you agree with her? Exchange opinions about the suspects in pairs.

> Wanda wanted his money. She murdered him! She murdered him because she was greedy.

A: I agree with Stella.
B: I disagree. I think Bob and Stella murdered Ivor because ...

5 Listen to the end of the story and check your answer.

Writing

A confession: *so* and *because*

6 Look at the examples.

Cause	Action
Wanda wanted his money	**so** she murdered him.

Action	Cause
She murdered him	**because** she was greedy.

7 Join sentence halves 1–4 and a–d.

1 Ivor knew that Hogg was dishonest
2 Stella loved Ivor
3 Hadley was preparing the food
4 The inspector found the answer

a so he recorded their conversation.
b because he was the cook.
c because he read the love letter.
d so she gave him a present.

8 Complete the murderer's confession with *so* and *because*.

> I murdered Ivor Bundell on 5th May 2002. I decided to do this about two months ago. I didn't like Mr Bundell **because** I thought that he was a mean and greedy person. I was also very jealous, **(1)** ...... I decided to murder him.
> I didn't know about chemistry, **(2)** ...... I studied books about chemicals and poisons. Then I went to town and I bought some chemical products. I made the poison a week ago. It wasn't difficult.
> The dinner party was a good time to use the poison **(3)** ...... there were a lot of people in the house. I put the poison in Mr Bundell's drink when he was in the kitchen. I forgot to hide the bottle of poison **(4)** ...... some people arrived. When the police arrived they found the bottle and my letter.

9 Detectives discovered that you stole a million-dollar diamond necklace. Write your confession. Use *so* and *because*, and include this information.

- Why did you do it?
- How, when and where did you do it?
- Who helped you?
- How did the police discover your identity?

Necklace robbery – suspect confesses!

Finished?

Think of a punishment for different crimes. Choose from:
- a fine.
- time in prison.

> My punishment for vandalism is a fine of £100.
> My punishment for murder is 30 years in prison.

Progress Check 2

Crimes

1 Write the names of the crimes.

drug dealer – drug dealing

1 kidnapper
2 murderer
3 robber
4 smuggler
5 vandal
6 pickpocket

Verbs

2 Match the verbs in the box with pictures 1–6.

plan   arrest   escape   hide   shoot   steal

1 plan

Past simple

3 Complete the dialogue with six words from the box.

did   ran   had   didn't   run   have   did   buy   bought

DI Fry: Why *did* you steal the football?
Adams: I (1) ...... steal it. I (2) ...... it.
DI Fry: Why (3) ...... you hide it under your jumper?
Adams: Because I didn't (4) ...... a bag.
DI Fry: And why did you (5) ...... down the street?
Adams: I (6) ...... because I needed the exercise.

Subject and object questions

4 Look at the diagram and write two questions for each person.

Who did Jack rob? Fran.
Who robbed Jack? Mary.

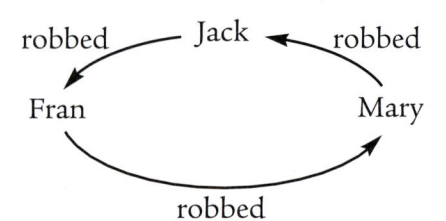

Jack — robbed → Fran
Mary — robbed → Jack
Fran — robbed → Mary

Past continuous

5 What were you doing at these times? Write sentences.

1 8 o'clock this morning
2 8 o'clock last night
3 2 o'clock yesterday afternoon
4 2 o'clock last night

Past simple and past continuous

6 Complete the sentences with correct forms of the past simple and the past continuous.

I was looking for a job and I decided to become a cook.

1 I ...... (work) in a big house when I ...... (find) some diamonds.
2 When I ...... (see) the diamonds, my boss ...... (talk) to her husband.
3 They ...... (watch TV) when I ...... (say) goodbye.
4 I ...... (sit) on a beach in Bermuda when the police ...... (find) me.

The World of English 1

North Street (pages 22 and 23)

Revision: present simple, present continuous, past simple, past continuous

Function: Making arrangements

1 Who's meeting Rick after school?

Culture File (pages 24 and 25)

Topic: International English

2 Where can you see this sign?

The Story of Pop (page 26)

Artist: Elvis Presley
Type: Rock and roll
Song: Blue suede shoes

3 When was Elvis Presley born?

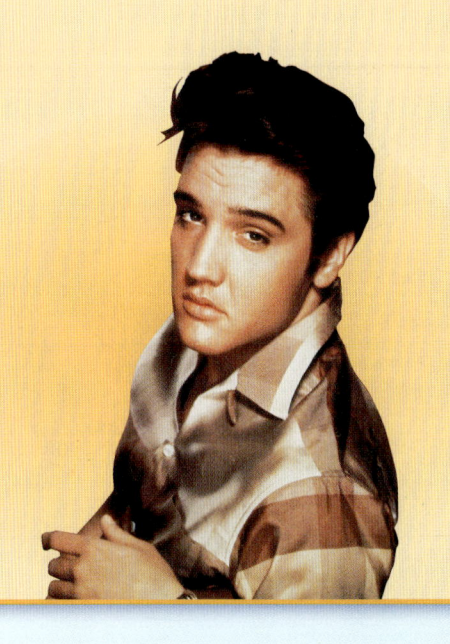

North Street

See you later!

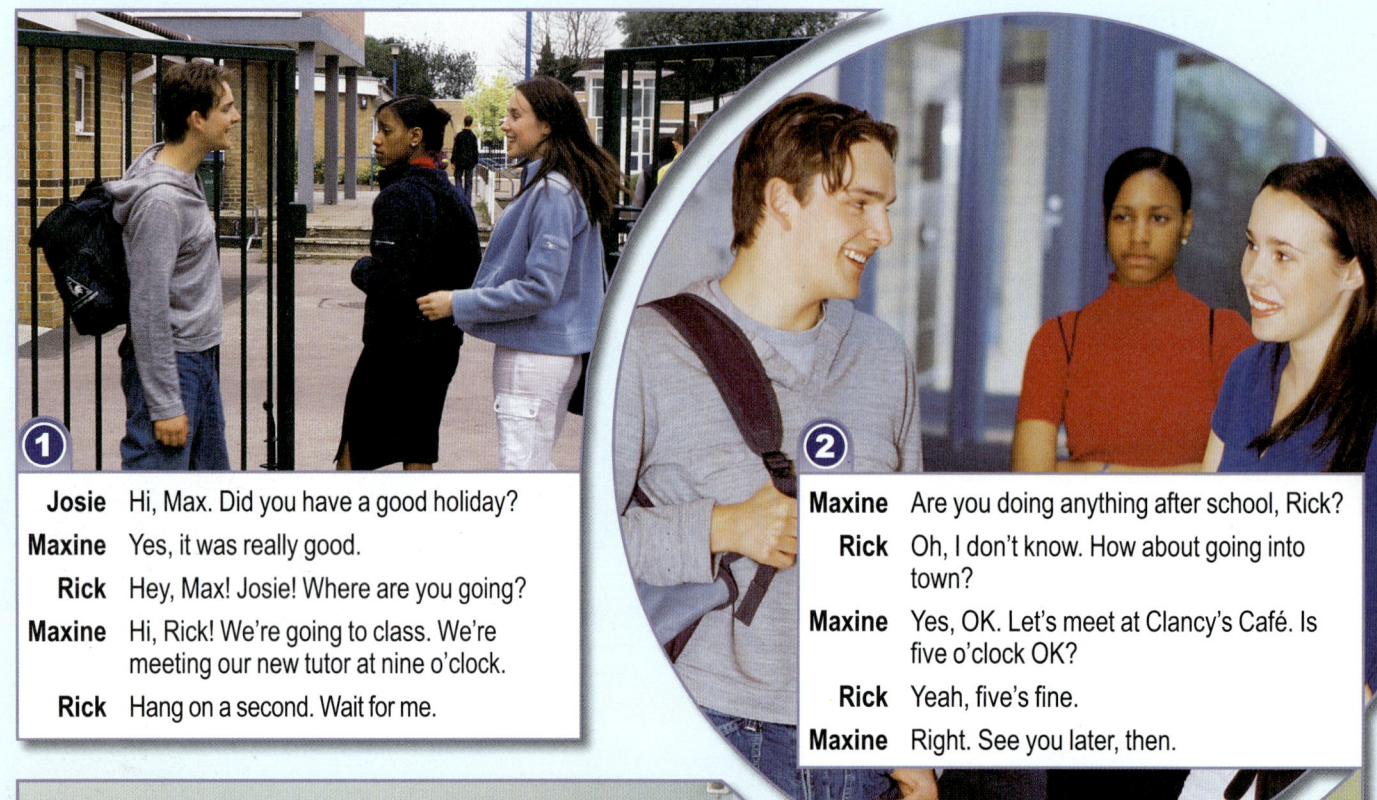

1

Josie	Hi, Max. Did you have a good holiday?
Maxine	Yes, it was really good.
Rick	Hey, Max! Josie! Where are you going?
Maxine	Hi, Rick! We're going to class. We're meeting our new tutor at nine o'clock.
Rick	Hang on a second. Wait for me.

2

Maxine	Are you doing anything after school, Rick?
Rick	Oh, I don't know. How about going into town?
Maxine	Yes, OK. Let's meet at Clancy's Café. Is five o'clock OK?
Rick	Yeah, five's fine.
Maxine	Right. See you later, then.

3 Later, in class …

Ms Rossi	OK? Now, have you got any questions for me?
Maxine	Yes, Ms Rossi. Which subject do you teach?
Ms Rossi	I teach Italian. I'm from Venezia.
Maxine	Vene-what? Oh … you're from Italy! You speak very good English.
Ms Rossi	Thanks. You, too!

4

Mr Daniels	Ms Rossi? Hi, I'm Pete Daniels … from the English department.
Ms Rossi	Oh, good morning. Nice to meet you. My name's Cristina.
Mr Daniels	How was your morning? Were you teaching?
Ms Rossi	Yes, I was. It was good. The students are friendly.
Mr Daniels	Mmm. We'll see, Cristina. We'll see.

Reading

1 **Read and listen to North Street. Then answer the questions.**

1. What are the names of the students in the story?
2. What are the names of the teachers?
3. What time are the students meeting after school?
4. Does Cristina teach English?
5. What does Cristina think of her new students?

Useful expressions

2 **Find the expressions in the story. Then check their meaning.**

1. Hang on a second.
2. See you later.
3. Nice to meet you.
4. We'll see.

Dialogue

Making arrangements

3 **Look at this extract from North Street. Listen and repeat. Concentrate on your rhythm and intonation.**

A: Are you doing anything *after school, Rick*?
B: Oh, I don't know. How about *going into town*?
A: Yes, OK. Let's meet *at Clancy's Café*. Is *five o'clock* OK?
B: Yeah, *five*'s fine.
A: Right. See you later, then.

4 **Make a list of possible activities for a Friday evening. Use the ideas in the pictures.**

1 go to a burger bar

5 **In pairs, discuss the ideas from exercise 4. Use exercise 3 as a model. Substitute the blue words to form your own dialogues.**

A: Are you doing anything on Friday evening, David?
B: Oh, I don't know. How about going to a burger bar?
A: Yes, OK. Let's meet at Megaburger. Is eight o'clock OK?
B: Yeah, eight's fine.
A: Right. See you later, then.

The World of English 1   23

Culture File 1

International English

1 Look at the photos. Where do you see English in your country?

International English

People use English around the world, from Australia to Zimbabwe and from Albania to Zaire. About 400 years ago, the number of English speakers in the world was probably between 5 and 7 million. There are now more than 500 million native speakers.

The USA has the biggest population of English speakers, but English is also the first language in Britain, Ireland, New Zealand, Canada, Australia and South Africa. China has got a bigger population than all of these places, but Mandarin Chinese is not an international language. Not many people speak Chinese outside China, but an enormous number of people study English as a foreign language.

But how did English become so important? There are three main reasons. Firstly, Britain colonized many countries. Secondly, some of those countries became very rich and powerful, especially the United States. Finally, international communication became very important, and in many situations we now need an international language.

English is the language of international business, politics, science, tourism and computers. If a Japanese company wants to talk to Arabic clients, they probably speak English.

2 Work in pairs. Discuss the questions.

When do you use English?

Do you find English easy to learn?

Is English important to you now? In the future?

Should we invent a new 'world language'?

3 Read the sentences and choose the correct words. Then read the text and check.

1 China has got a **bigger** / **smaller** population than the United States.

2 English is the **first** / **second** language in Australia.

3 **English** / **Japanese** is the language of computers.

4 **Some** / **Most** information on the internet is in English.

5 The English language **is** / **isn't** changing.

Doctors, students, engineers and businessmen study English so that they can communicate with colleagues and friends in other countries. 70% of scientists write in English and 80% of information on the internet is also in English.

In the future, English will probably continue to be the most important international language. The number of speakers is increasing very fast, and the language is also growing and changing. Who knows, perhaps in the future English will become simpler and easier to learn!

4 **Look at pictures a–d. Listen to three of these people talking and answer the questions.**

1 Which of the people do you hear?
2 Which of the people are easy to understand?
3 Which of the people are difficult to understand?

a Hatsue   b Claudia   c Rob   d Ivan

5 **Listen again and complete the table.**

	1	2	3
Name	Rob		
Nationality			
Where do they study English?			
Why do they study English?			

Project

Find something in English that you really like. Use the ideas in the box or think of your own.

> a web page   a recipe   a song
> a book   a magazine   a video
> a computer game   an advert

Show it to the class and talk about it. Think about:

- where you found it.
- what it's about.
- why you like it.

The World of English 1

The Story of Pop 1

Rock and roll

1 Read and listen. Then answer the questions.

1 What type of music became 'rock and roll'?
2 What adjectives describe rock and roll?
3 What did the police try to stop at rock and roll concerts?
4 What adjectives describe Elvis Presley?
5 How old was Elvis when he died?

2 Complete the song with a–e. Then listen and check.

a fruit jar
b my house
c car
d my shoes
e liquor

Rock and roll

Popular music at the end of the 1940s was slow and traditional. Then, black musicians in the USA started to play strong, exciting 'rhythm and blues' music. Soon, radio disc jockeys (DJs) started to play rhythm and blues, and one DJ, Alan Freed, called it 'rock and roll'.

Teenagers loved rock and roll immediately because it was fast, fun and young. In the 1950s, the police tried to stop teenagers dancing at rock and roll concerts.

Alan Freed

Elvis Presley

Elvis was born in 1935. When he was young, he learned to sing in church, and he played the guitar and the piano. He was shy, but he was also very ambitious. His first records weren't big hits, but he soon became the most popular rock and roll singer in the world.

In the five days after Elvis died in 1977, people bought 8 million of his records! Today, people still call him 'the King' of rock and roll.

Blue suede shoes

(Chorus)
Well, it's one for the money,
Two for the show,
Three to get ready,
Now go, cat, go.
But don't you step on my blue suede shoes.
You can do anything, but don't touch my blue suede shoes.

Well, you can knock me down,
Step on my face,
Slander my name
All over the place.
Do anything that you want to do, but uh-uh,
Honey, don't touch my shoes.
Don't you step on my blue suede shoes.
You can do anything, but don't touch my blue suede shoes.

You can burn (1) ...b...,
Steal my (2) ...c...,
Drink my (3) ...e...
From an old (4) ...a... .
Do anything that you want to do, but uh-uh,
Honey, don't touch (5) ...d...
Don't you step on my blue suede shoes.
You can do anything, but don't touch my blue suede shoes!

(Repeat chorus)

Glossary
liquor (USA) = alcohol (UK)

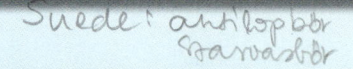

3 Tasty!

Have a look!

Find the pages where you:
- read about healthy eating.
- listen to people talking about a theme restaurant.
- write a recipe.

Vocabulary

Food

1 Match the words in the box with food items 1–10. Then listen and check.

> tuna   ham   mushroom   pineapple
> prawn   sweetcorn   olive   onion
> pepper   egg

1 sweetcorn

2 What other things do you like on your pizza?

Speaking

3 Work in pairs. Ask and answer questions about your likes and dislikes. Use the expressions in the box.

> Yes, lots.   No, not much.   No, not at all.

A: Do you like olives?
B: No, not much.

VOCABULARY PAGE 125, 3.1

3a Hard Rock Café

Listening

Tina Hall presents a consumer programme on TV. She is interviewing Mick and Ruth at the Hard Rock Café, a theme restaurant in London.

1 Listen and complete the notes.

Restaurant: Hard Rock Café

	Points
Atmosphere	10/10
Food	(1) /10
Service / staff	(2) /10
Price	(3) /10
Total points =	(4) /40

2 Listen again and complete the sentences.

Atmosphere
There are interesting things everywhere, like *gold discs and musical instruments*
1 We didn't see anybody ......

Food
2 Is there anything for ......?
3 Everything was very ......

Service
4 Everybody here is friendly, but ......
5 We didn't eat anything until ......

Price
6 We both bought something – these ......

Exploring grammar

Pronouns: *some...*, *any...* and *every...*

3 Complete the table with words from exercise 2.

	some...	any...	every...
Places	somewhere	anywhere	*everywhere*
Things	something	(1)	(2) ......
People	somebody	anybody	(3) ......

4 Look at the examples. Do we use *any* in affirmative sentences?

1 We didn't see anybody famous.
2 There isn't anything strange on the menu.
3 Did you buy anything?

GRAMMAR PAGE 117

5 Complete the dialogue. Use the words in the box.

> everywhere ~~something~~ anything
> everything everybody anywhere

Lady: Excuse me, I need *something* to eat.
Chef: Well, we've got (1) ...... on the menu.
Lady: It's all burgers. Is there (2) ...... for vegetarians?
Chef: No, but (3) ...... loves our burgers.
Lady: I don't. Is there good food (4) ...... in this town?
Chef: No, (5) ...... is closed, except my brother's burger bar near the station.

6 Look at the photo. Complete the pronouns. Then invent answers.

Alcatraz BC theme restaurant, Tokyo, Japan

Is there a similar restaurant any*where* in the world?

No, there isn't.

1 Does any...... famous come here?
2 Is there ......thing interesting on the walls?
3 Is every...... happy with the service?
4 What happens when some...... complains?
5 Please recommend ......thing from the menu.

Pronunciation
Silent vowels

7 Listen and repeat.

Silent vowel(s)	No silent vowels
1 int<u>e</u>resting	3 excellent
2 om<u>e</u>lette	4 visiting

8 Add words 1–4 to the table in exercise 7. <u>Underline</u> the silent vowels. Then listen and check.

1 theme
2 chocolate
3 vegetable
4 atmosphere

Speaking

9 Think of a name for a new restaurant. Then ask and answer questions from exercise 6.

A: *Tell me about your restaurant.*
B: *It's called Anna's Food Palace.*
A: *Is there a similar restaurant anywhere in the world?*
B: *No, of course there isn't.*

Vocabulary
Preparing food: verbs and adjectives

10 Match the verbs with the adjectives.

bake – baked

Verbs		Adjectives	
~~bake~~	boil	grilled	fried
freeze	fry	roast	boiled
grill	roast	frozen	~~baked~~

11 Complete the descriptions. Use the adjectives from exercise 10.

1   2   3
4   5   6

1 *baked* potato   4 ...... onion
2 ...... sardines   5 ...... vegetables
3 ...... eggs   6 ...... chicken

VOCABULARY PAGE 125, 3.2

Finished?

Write about your food preferences.
I love roast chicken and chips. I hate ...

Unit 3 *Tasty!* **29**

3b Food, fat and fibre

Reading

1 Do the Food Test. Then read the Food Facts and check your answers.

The Food Test

How much do you know about food and nutrition? Do you know what's good and what's bad for you?

1. How much fat is there in sausages?
   a a lot   b not much
2. How many vitamins are there in fresh vegetables?
   a a lot   b not many
3. Are protein and fibre good for you?
   a yes   b no
4. Are fat and cholesterol bad for you?
   a yes   b no

2 Read the text again and answer the questions.

1. Is it OK to eat three eggs every day?
2. Which potato products contain salt and fat?
3. Which is healthier, sausage or tuna?
4. What should you eat if you've got a sweet tooth?
5. Which three things contain a lot of vitamins?

Look!
Countable and uncountable nouns

Countable	Uncountable
eggs sweets potatoes	salt sugar fat

GRAMMAR PAGE 118

Food Facts

Eggs
Eggs contain vitamins and protein, but they also contain cholesterol. Cholesterol isn't very good for you, but it's OK to eat three or four eggs a week.

Potatoes
Potatoes are OK, but beware of chips and crisps! Chips and crisps aren't good for your heart because they often contain extra salt and extra fat.

Fish and seafood
Fish and seafood are good for you. Tuna, for example, is rich in protein and there isn't much fat in it.

Salad and vegetables
Salad and fresh vegetables are really good for you. There are a lot of vitamins and fibre in them, and they're delicious! Are there enough vegetables in your diet?

Sausages
Don't eat too many sausages. There's a lot of fat in them, and they aren't a very healthy food.

Chocolates and sweets
Chocolates and sweets don't contain much fibre or protein, but they've got a lot of sugar in them. Too much sugar is bad for your teeth. Fruit is better if you want a snack.

Fruit
There's some sugar in fruit, but it isn't bad for you. Fresh fruit is excellent because it contains a lot of vitamins. People don't eat enough fruit.

3b

Exploring grammar
Quantity: *a lot of*, *many* and *much*

3 Look at the table and answer the questions.
1 Which words can we **only** use with uncountable nouns?
2 Which words can we **only** use with countable nouns?
3 Which words can we use with **both** countable nouns **and** uncountable nouns?

Countable	Uncountable
How many …?	How much …?
a lot of	a lot of
some	some
not many	not much
not any	not any

GRAMMAR PAGE 118

4 Complete the questions with *How much* and *How many*. Then choose answers from the box.

> 18 litres   0.2 litres   100 grams   1
> ~~None~~   1 or 2

How much sugar is there on the table? None.
1 …… juice is there?
2 …… packets of cereal are there on the table?
3 …… marmalade is there in the jar?
4 …… eggs can a chicken produce in a day?
5 …… milk can a cow produce in a day?

5 Write about your diet. Use the words from exercise 3 and some of the words in the box.

> burgers   cheese   chips   coffee
> doughnuts   meat   milk   sweets   water

I don't drink much milk.
I eat a lot of cheese.

(not) enough, too much and too many

6 Translate sentences 1–4.
1 Are there **enough** vegetables in your diet?
2 Don't eat **too many** sausages.
3 **Too much** sugar is bad for you.
4 People don't eat **enough** fruit.

GRAMMAR PAGE 118

7 Bob went shopping. Look at the shopping list and the picture. Write sentences with *enough*, *not enough*, *too much* and *too many*.

He bought too much cheese.
He didn't buy enough eggs.

1 milk   3 bananas   5 peppers
2 juice   4 pizzas

Shopping list
250 grams cheese ✓
12 eggs ✓
1 litre milk
1 litre juice
4 bananas
1 pizza
2 peppers

Finished?

Make a *healthy* shopping list and an *unhealthy* shopping list.
Healthy – water, vegetables

Unit 3 *Tasty!*

3c Strange tastes

Reading

1 Read and listen. How many different insects does the text mention?

Strange tastes

How do you prefer your ants? Boiled or fried? It's a strange question, but in fact people eat insects in a lot of different countries. In Australia, for example, the Aborigines eat ants. Ants are also a delicacy in Ecuador. People eat grasshoppers in Nigeria and also in restaurants in Tokyo. In Mexico, insects are very popular: people eat 200 different types of insect!

But why eat insects? There are four very good reasons:

- there are a lot of them;
- they're cheap;
- they're good for you; and
- they can be tasty!

In some countries it is difficult to find food that contains enough vitamins and protein. Often people haven't got much money, or there isn't any food. Insects are an ideal solution. There are millions and millions of insects, and they contain a lot of vitamins and protein.

Perhaps you think that eating insects is horrible, but the idea is becoming more popular in Europe and the USA. You can now buy insect recipe books, and in New York City, there's an insect restaurant! So if you find a fly in your soup, don't complain – ask for more!

Recipe for baked crickets (USA)
1. First, wash 10 crickets.
2. Then, freeze them for 30 minutes.
3. After that, bake the crickets in an oven at 200°C for 90 minutes.
4. Finally, serve the crickets with salt and a mixed salad.

2 Read the text again. Write *True*, *False* or *I don't know* for sentences 1–5.

People eat grasshoppers in Ecuador.
I don't know.

1 Insects are popular in Mexico.
2 Insects are very expensive.
3 Insects contain cholesterol.
4 Insect dishes are becoming popular.
5 There's an insect restaurant in the USA.

Writing

Cooking instructions: *first, then, after that* and *finally*

3 Read the recipe for baked crickets in exercise 1 again. Then put pictures a–d in order.

1b

4 Read the recipe for scorpions in chocolate. Rewrite the recipe in order. Include *first, then, after that,* and *finally*.

Recipe for scorpions in chocolate (China)

a ......, heat some chocolate.

b ......, put the scorpions on some kitchen paper and eat them when they are cold.

c *First*, bake some scorpions.

d ......, dip each scorpion in the chocolate.

Study skills

Brainstorming vocabulary

You are going to write a recipe. It is always a good idea to think about vocabulary before you write.

5 Complete the lists with the words in the box.

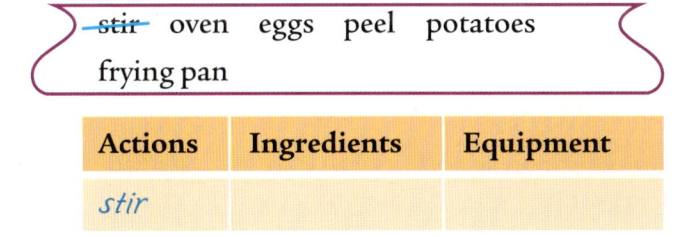

~~stir~~ oven eggs peel potatoes frying pan

Actions	Ingredients	Equipment
stir		

6 Think of the vocabulary you need for your recipe and add it to the table in exercise 5. Use a dictionary.

7 Write your recipe. Use *first, then, after that* and *finally* and your words from exercise 6.

Spanish omelette
First peel three potatoes ...

Finished?

Invent an exotic dinner menu.

First course	Main course	Dessert
Baked crickets	......	......

Unit 3 *Tasty!*

Progress Check 3

Food

1 Complete the words.

Meat	Fish / Seafood	Vegetables
1 sausage	3 p_ _ _ _ _	5 o_ _ _ _
2 h_ _	4 t_ _ _	6 p_ _ _ _ _

Preparing food: verbs and adjectives

2 Write words for sentences 1–4.

Apples cooked in the oven. *baked apples*

1 Chicken cooked in the oven.
2 Potatoes cooked in very hot water.
3 Fish cooked on a barbecue.
4 Fish cooked in oil in a pan.

Pronouns: *some…*, *any…* and *every…*

3 Complete the text with the words in the box.

> everybody   something   anybody
> everything   ~~anything~~   anything

SPACE FOOD – an interview with an astronaut

What do people eat in space? Is *anything* different?
In the past the food wasn't good. Most food was in tubes and (1) …… complained. Now spacecraft are bigger, so we can take (2) …… fresh, usually fruit.

Is it difficult to eat in space?
In space (3) …… floats because there is zero gravity so food is in special containers.

Does (4) …… cook in space?
There is an oven on the space shuttle, but astronauts don't prepare (5) ……. They add water to the food and heat it.

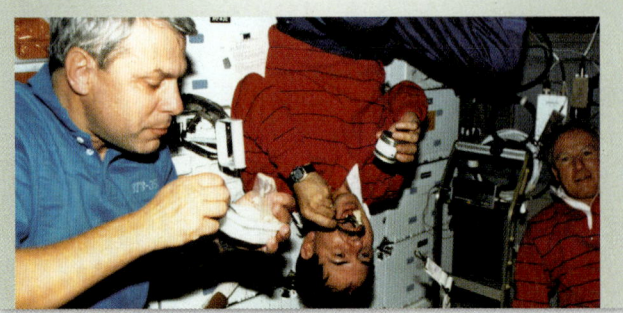

Quantity: *a lot of*, *many* and *much*

4 Complete the text with *a lot of*, *many* and *much*.

The Story of Pizza

- Not *many* people know that the ancient Greeks made a dish similar to pizza called 'plankuntos'.
- In Italy, people didn't use (1) …… cheese on pizzas 150 years ago. Cheese was too expensive.
- When Queen Margherita of Italy visited Naples (Napoli) in 1889, a baker called Rafael Esposito invented a pizza for her. It didn't have (2) …… ingredients: herbs, cheese and tomato. The pizza was the colours of the Italian flag: green, white and red.
- The first pizzeria in the USA opened in 1905. For many years, there weren't (3) …… pizzerias outside Italy, but in the 1940s, (4) …… American soldiers passed through Italy and they 'discovered' pizza! Now there are pizzerias all over the world.
- For perfect results, put fresh herbs and olive oil on your pizza before you bake it. You don't need (5) …… oil, but it is an important ingredient.

(not) *enough*, *too much* and *too many*

5 Write sentences about the restaurant. Use *enough*, *not enough*, *too much* and *too many*.

There are enough serviettes.

| 1 chairs | 3 food | 5 chips |
| 2 waiters | 4 glasses | 6 water |

A table for two

4 Buy and sell

Have a look!

Find the pages where you:
- listen to people talking about buying shoes.
- plan an advert.
- do a consumer quiz.

Vocabulary

Shopping

1 Match the words in the box with pictures 1–8. Then listen and check.

> advert   customer   ~~logo~~   price   shelf
> shop assistant   slogan   special offer

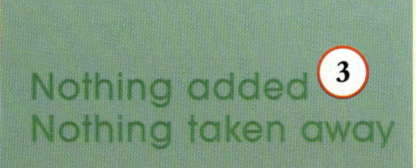

1 logo

Speaking

2 Ask and answer the questions.

1 Which shops in your area have the most customers?
2 Do you wear clothes with logos on them?
3 What do you think of the price of trainers and computer games?
4 Can you describe any adverts from TV or magazines?
5 Can you remember any slogans from adverts?

> VOCABULARY   PAGE 125, 4.1

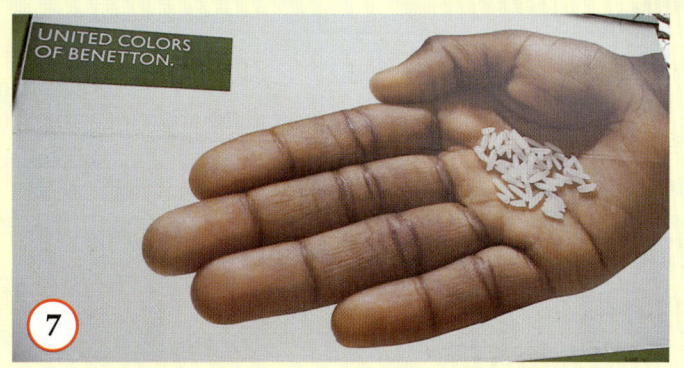

35

4a In the supermarket

Reading

1 Do the quiz and check your score.

Consumer Quiz

Do you know the secrets of the supermarket?

Imagine that you are the manager of a big supermarket. Choose answer a or b for each question.

1 Do you play music in your supermarket?
   a Yes. People are more relaxed when they listen to music – they stay in the shop and they buy more.
   b No. Music is the least important thing in a shop.

2 Where do you sell flowers, fresh fruit and vegetables?
   a Near the entrance. They're more attractive than packets and boxes. People are happier when they see the flowers. Happy customers spend more money.
   b Near the exit, then people feel happy when they go home.

3 What type of people work in your shop?
   a The friendliest, smartest people. The customers are happier if shop assistants are friendly.
   b Young people are the best because they are the fastest. They can serve more customers.

4 Where do you put the most expensive products, or the products that you really want to sell?
   a At eye level. 'Eye level is buy level!'
   b I put the most expensive products on the highest shelf. Then people can't steal them.

5 Which colours do you prefer on the packets and cans in your shop?
   a Bright colours are the most attractive for customers. Red, yellow, orange and blue are the best colours because they are brighter. Dull colours are less attractive.
   b I think that other things are more important than the colour of the packet.

What's your score?

2 points for each **a** answer. 1 point for each **b** answer.

5–6 Oh, dear. Not a very good score. Your shop won't survive. What were your bad decisions?

7–8 Not bad, but you need to learn more about shops, or you'll have problems.

9–10 Excellent! You obviously know the secrets of the supermarket. Your shop will be very successful!

Exploring grammar
Comparative and superlative adjectives

2 Complete the table with the comparative or superlative form of the adjectives in exercise 1.

Regular adjectives

Adjective	Comparative	Superlative
fast	faster	(1) ......
friendly	friendlier	(2) ......
attractive	(3)	the most attractive
important	less important	(4) ......

Irregular adjectives

Adjective	Comparative	Superlative
bad	worse	the worst
good	better	(5) ......

GRAMMAR ▶ PAGE 119

3 Compare the products.

Bubbles is cheaper than D-Lish.

1 Wizz / expensive / D-Lish.
2 The D-Lish can / bright / the Wizz can.
3 The D-Lish offer / good / the Bubbles offer.
4 The D-Lish can / big / the Bubbles can.
5 The Bubbles can / attractive / the Wizz can.

4 Write sentences about the products.

Bubbles is the cheapest.

Vocabulary
Adjectives

5 Find pairs of opposites. Then listen and check.

big   bright   cheap   dangerous   dull
expensive   fast   unfashionable   heavy
fashionable   safe   slow   small   light

big – small

VOCABULARY PAGE 125, 4.2

6 Write puzzle sentences about the products. Use the comparative and superlative forms of the adjectives in exercise 4.

It's slower than the scooter. (bicycle)
It's the lightest. (ring)

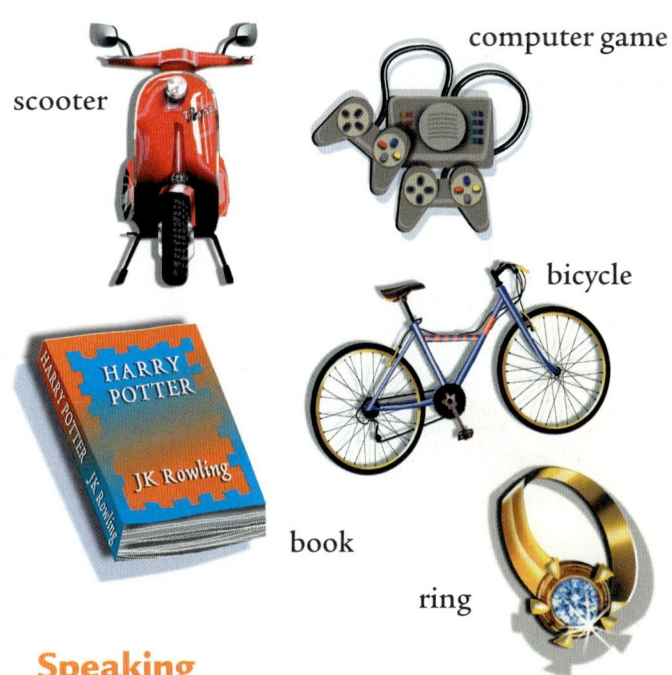

scooter   computer game   bicycle   book   ring

Speaking

7 Read your sentences from exercise 5 to your partner. Guess your partner's products.

Finished?

Write about products that you know.
The best trainers are ...
The worst car is ...

4b Shopping

Listening

1 Look at the picture. Sandra wants to buy some shoes. What do you think John is saying?

2 Listen and look at the picture. Which shoes does Sandra want to buy – a, b or c?

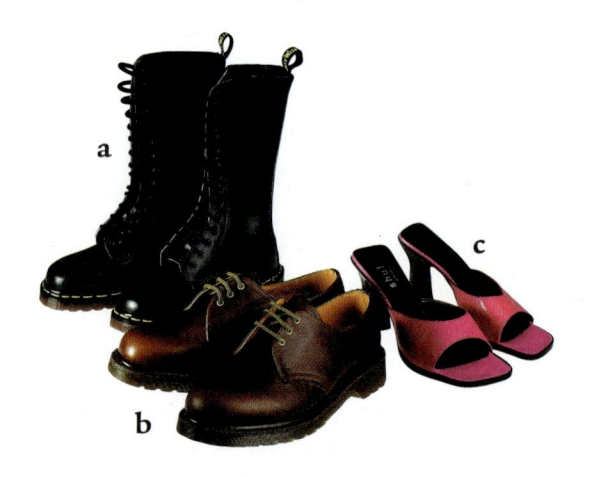

3 Listen again and answer the questions.
1. Where does John want to go?
2. Why does Sandra want to buy some shoes?
3. What does Sandra think of the boots?
4. Which shoes does John suggest?
5. John says that Sandra will need sunglasses. Why?
6. When is Sandra going to visit the shop again?

Exploring grammar

going to and *will*

4 Complete the rules with *going to* or *will*.

> I'**m going to** look in this shop.
> I'**m going to** come here again tomorrow.
> I'm sure they **won't** be cheap.
> People **will** laugh at me.
>
> We use ...... to talk about a plan or intention for the future.
>
> We use ...... to talk about a prediction about the future.
>
> We often use **will** with:
> probably, maybe, I (don't) think ..., I'm sure ...

> GRAMMAR ▶ PAGE 119

5 Complete the dialogue with the correct form of *going to* or *will*.

> **SHOPPING CITY COMPETITION**
>
> Congratulations! You are the lucky winner.
> Your prize – Visit three shops and take one thing from each shop **FREE!**

Sue: Your brother won that competition! When *is* he *going to go* (go) to town?

Tom: On Saturday. He's planned everything. He (**1**) ...... (find) a new computer.

Sue: Wow! And then what?

Tom: I think he (**2**) ...... (get) me a present.

Sue: Really? What present?

Tom: I'm not sure. We (**3**) ...... probably ...... (look) at the DVD players.

Sue: There's another competition next week. I've decided I (**4**) ...... (enter) it.

Tom: Oh well, good luck! Maybe you (**5**) ...... (win).

Sue: Thanks. I hope so.

4b

6 Look at exercise 5 again. Imagine that you are the prize winner. Answer the questions. Use complete sentences.

1. When are you going to collect your prizes?
2. Which three shops are you going to visit?
3. Which shop are you going to go to first?
4. Are you going to look for presents for people?
5. What will your friends probably say when you tell them?
6. Who do you think will want to go with you?
7. Do you think you'll be in the newspaper?
8. Do you think you'll enter another competition?

too and (not) ... enough

7 Study the examples.

> They're smart **enough**.
> They are**n't** bright **enough**.
> They're **too** expensive.

GRAMMAR ➤ PAGE 120

8 Write sentences with *too* and *(not) ... enough*.

New trainers (size 44)   Andy's trainers (size 41)

Andy's trainers are too old.

1. Andy's trainers / smart
2. they / unfashionable
3. they / bright
4. the new trainers / expensive
5. they / cheap for Andy
6. they / big for Andy

9 Complete the dialogue with lines a–d. Then listen and check.

Ben: Let's buy a present for Joseph.
Mel: (1) ....
Ben: What about a new watch?
Mel: (2) ....
Ben: Well, what about a pen?
Mel: (3) ....
Ben: OK. Let's get a CD.
Mel: (4) ....

a No, that's not exciting enough.
b Good idea!
c No, watches are too expensive.
d OK. What shall we buy?

Pronunciation
Intonation

10 Listen and repeat. Are the speakers positive or negative?

1. What about a new watch? *Positive*
2. Watches are too expensive. *Negative*
3. That's not exciting enough.
4. OK. Let's get a CD.

11 Practise the dialogue from exercise 9. Concentrate on your intonation.

Speaking

12 Change the blue words in the dialogue in exercise 9. Then in pairs, practise the new dialogue.

> A: Let's buy a present for Alex.
> B: OK. What shall we buy?
> A: What about a new T-shirt?

Finished?

Write a 'dream' shopping list.
1 motorbike

Unit 4 *Buy and sell* 39

4c Adverts

Reading

1 Read and listen. Choose headings for paragraphs 1–5 from the box.

1b

- **a** Adverts of the future
- **b** Introduction
- **c** Cows and ice cream
- **d** Old and new methods
- **e** Fashion symbols
- **f** The first adverts

Advertising

1 Adverts are everywhere. A good advert uses the best words and the best images in the best place. But where do you hear and see these images?

2 We often see or hear adverts on television and radio, in newspapers and magazines, at the cinema and on posters. But companies are always looking for more imaginative ideas, and they are now starting to put adverts in more unusual places. We now see the names of products all around us – on tables, taxis or in the sky! This idea is called 'ambient' advertising.

3 One ice cream company called Ben and Jerry's, had a very original idea. They produced some plastic 'jackets' for cows and they put the name of their company on the jackets. Then they paid a farmer to put the jackets on his cows. The farmer's field was next to a motorway and thousands of people saw the jackets. The farmer was happy, the ice cream company was happy, and the cows were warm!

4 People also wear adverts. Sports stars receive a fortune when they use a company's product or wear clothes with company logos. People like to wear the most fashionable symbols on expensive clothes, or even in their hair!

5 There are always new or unusual places for adverts. In 2000, a Russian rocket went into space with the name of a pizza restaurant on its side. It was the first advert in space and there are plans for more. In the future when we look at the sky at night we'll see the moon, the stars and an advert for cola.

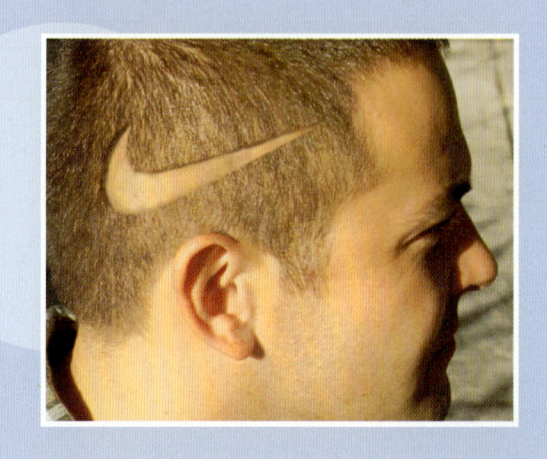

4c

2 Read the text again and answer the questions.
1. What are three normal places for adverts?
2. What's the name of a new type of advertising?
3. Why do sports stars wear company logos?
4. Why do other people wear logos?
5. Where will we see more adverts in the future?

Listening

3 Look at the pictures and listen to adverts for the products. Which products do you hear?

4 Complete the information from the adverts with the words in the box. Then listen and check.

> new   you   Delicious   ~~colours~~
> colourful   high   wind   cool   whiter

With new Radiant your *colours* are more (**1**) ......, and your whites are (**2**) ...... than white. Because with Radiant everything's as good as (**3**) ....

Rockard (**4**) ...... technology trainers. They're as light as a feather, so you can run like the (**5**) ....

(**6**) ...... white chocolate and cool, (**7**) ...... ice cream. Choc D'or. It's new, it's for (**8**) ...... and it tastes like paradise.

Writing
Planning an advert: *than, as ... as ..., like*

5 Translate the slogans.

than	1	whiter than white
as ... as ...	2	as light as a feather
like	3	It tastes like paradise.

6 Match 1–6 with a–f.
1. It works — a ... like an angel.
2. This is harder — b ... than lightning.
3. He's got a face — c ... than steel.
4. It's faster — d ... like a dream.
5. I'm as free — e ... as ice.
6. The room was as cold — f ... as a bird.

7 Imagine that you want to advertise one of the products in the box. Write about your plans. Include your answers to the questions.

> a car   a magazine   a perfume   a drink

- What's the name of your product?
- Who is the product for?
- Why do you think people will buy your product?
- Where are you going to advertise?
- What famous people are going to appear in the advert?
- What music are you going to use?
- Describe the advert. What images are you going to use?

Finished?
Invent a logo and a slogan for your product.

Petal – It's as fresh as a daisy!

Unit 4 *Buy and sell*

Progress Check 4

Shopping

1 Complete the text with the words in the box.

> adverts   prices   shelves   slogan
> shop assistants   customers   special offers

Scott's
WE'RE SIMPLY THE BEST!

Here at Scott's supermarket our friendly *shop assistants* always try to help, because we think that our (1) …… are important. We've also got the best products on our (2) …… and our (3) …… are the lowest in town. Listen to our (4) …… on the radio, with information about our fantastic (5) ……! Scott's – remember our (6) …… : 'We're simply the best!'

Adjectives

2 Write the opposites of the adjectives.

light – *heavy*
1 bright
2 fast
3 fashionable
4 safe
5 expensive

Comparative and superlative adjectives

3 Write about the objects. Use the comparative form of the adjectives.

A car is noisier than a skateboard.

> intelligent   big   fast   small   noisy
> expensive

- a skateboard
- a house
- a dog
- a hamster
- a ring
- a car

4 Write five sentences about the objects. Use the superlative form of the adjectives.

A ring is the smallest object.

going to and *will*

5 Complete the dialogue with the correct forms of *going to* and *will*.

The World of English 2

North Street (pages 44 and 45)

Revision: *going to, will, (not) … enough,* comparatives
Function: Shopping

1. What is the problem with Rick's alarm clock?

Culture File (pages 46 and 47)

Topic: A multiracial society

2. What language does Anand speak at home?

The Story of Pop (page 48)

Artist: Martha Reeves
Type of music: Soul
Song: Nowhere to run

3. What church did Martha Reeves sing in?

North Street

You'll be late!

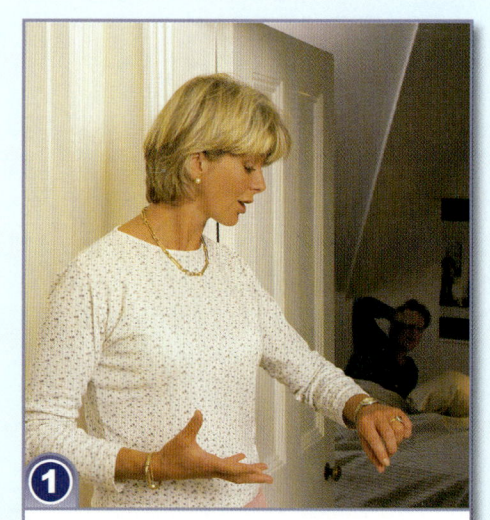

1

Rick's mum	Rick! It's half past eight.
Rick	What?
Rick's mum	I said it's half past eight. You'll be late!
Rick	Oh, no, not again. I don't believe it!

2

Ms Rossi	Rick! The class finished ten minutes ago!
Rick	Sorry I'm late, Ms Rossi. My alarm clock isn't loud enough.
Josie	Yeah, yeah! Typical Rick. Was there a match on TV last night?
Ms Rossi	OK. That's enough, thank you, Josie. Rick, that's three times this week.

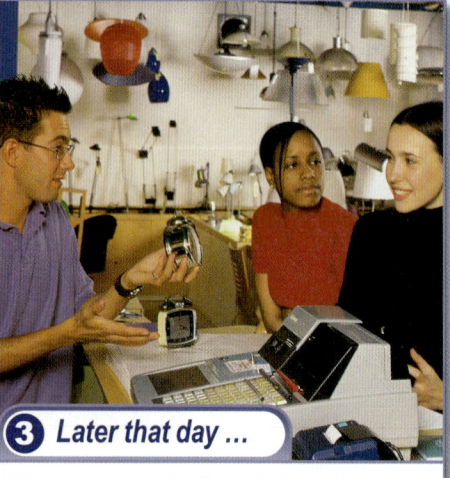

3 Later that day ...

Shop assistant	Can I help you?
Maxine	Yes, I'm looking for an alarm clock.
Shop assistant	Well, we've got some for £6.50.
Maxine	Have you got anything louder?
Shop assistant	Louder? Yes, of course. This one's £8.
Maxine	Great! I'll have that one, thanks.

4 The next day ...

Maxine	Hey, Rick. We bought a present for you. We think you'll like it.
Rick	A present? Thanks, Max. That's very kind of you.
Maxine	You're welcome. Sweet dreams, Rick!
Rick	Now what's this? Some chocolates ... or some ... hey! Josie! Maxine!

Reading

1 Read and listen to North Street. Then answer the questions.

1. What time did Rick wake up?
2. Did he miss the class?
3. Does Josie believe Rick's excuse?
4. What did the girls buy for Rick?
5. How much did the present cost?

Useful expressions

2 Find the expressions in the story. Then check their meaning.

1. Sorry I'm late.
2. That's enough.
3. That's very kind of you.
4. Sweet dreams.

Dialogue

Shopping

3 Look at this extract from North Street. Listen and repeat. Concentrate on your rhythm and intonation.

A: Can I help you?
B: Yes, I'm looking for an alarm clock.
A: Well, we've got some for £6.50.
B: Have you got anything louder?
A: Louder? Yes, of course. This one's £8.
B: Great! I'll have that one, thanks.

4 Imagine that you are shopping. Which of these things do you want to buy?

1. a mountain bike (£250 / big – £280)
2. a computer (£500 / cheap – £100)
3. a guitar (£100 / loud – £150)
4. a jacket (£35 / expensive – £95)

5 In pairs, discuss the ideas for shopping in exercise 4. Use exercise 3 as a model. Substitute the blue words to form your own dialogues.

A: Can I help you?
B: Yes, I'm looking for a mountain bike.
A: Well, we've got some for £250.
B: Have you got anything bigger?
A: Bigger? Yes, of course. This one's £280.
B: Great! I'll have that one, thanks.

The World of English 2

Culture File 2

Multiracial societies

1 Discuss the questions.

1 Do many people come from other countries to live in your country?
2 What do you know about their countries, religions and customs?

2 Read the text and complete the notes.

	Country	Languages	Religion	Religious building
Josie's family	Barbados	English		
Jamila's family				
Anand's family				

3 Complete the table with words from the text.

Religion	Person
Christianity	(1) ......
(2)	Muslim
Hinduism	(3) ......

Multiracial Britain

People from many different countries and cultures live in Britain: it's a multiracial society. Here, three British teenagers from different races talk about their families, languages and religions.

Josie

My grandparents came to Britain from Barbados in the 1960s when there was a lot of work here. They've got a strong Caribbean accent when they speak English, but my accent is from this area. I'm happy about that because I don't like to be different.

My parents are Christians and they go to a church called the 'New Testament Church of God'. Black people started the church about 30 years ago because they didn't feel at home in the churches here in Britain.

Jamila

My grandfather came here from Pakistan in 1953 when he saw adverts in newspapers there for jobs in Britain. I speak English most of the time, but I have to speak Urdu with my mother because her English is terrible. Urdu is the official language of Pakistan.

My family are Muslim so our religion is Islam. We pray five times a day wherever we are. It doesn't matter if we aren't in the mosque – Islam says that the whole world is a mosque because you can pray to God anywhere. However, every Saturday I go to the mosque to learn to read Arabic and to recite the Qur'an, our holy book.

Anand

My parents are from India. We speak English fluently, but when we're at home we speak an Indian language called Gujarati.

In the Hindu religion we believe that God has many forms, and people pray to different gods and goddesses. We have a small shrine in our house, a special place with pictures of the gods and goddesses. Every day we pray here and offer things such as fruit, rice, flowers, milk and water. We can also go to our local temple to pray and to celebrate festivals like Divali.

46

4 A guide is talking about a tour of New York. Listen and number the pictures in the order they are mentioned.

Join us on a tour of multicultural New York City!

a Little Italy during the San Gennaro celebrations

b A music club in Harlem

c The Immigration Museum on Ellis Island

d Street stalls in Chinatown

5 Listen again and answer the questions.
1. Why is New York a multicultural city?
2. How many immigrants arrived on Ellis Island between 1892 and 1954?
3. Is the Statue of Liberty on Ellis Island?
4. When is the feast of San Gennaro?
5. What is happening to Harlem now?
6. How many restaurants are there in Chinatown?

Project

Make a poster or leaflet about an interesting town or city. Include information about:

- things to see.
- things to do.
- typical food.
- any festivals / special events.

Include photos or drawings.

The World of English 2

The Story of Pop 2

Soul

1 Read and listen. Then answer the questions.

1. What adjectives describe gospel music?
2. Who developed soul music?
3. Where did Martha Reeves first sing?
4. What was Martha's first job at Motown?
5. Why did Martha first sing at the Motown studios?

2 Complete the song with the words in the box. Then listen and check.

> take   met   go   forget   look   know

Soul

Music is often an important part of religious celebration. Music in the Pentecostal church is particularly rhythmic and expressive. It's called 'gospel' music.

In the USA in the 1950s and 1960s, gospel was a big influence on black musicians. They adapted the rhythms and styles of gospel to create 'soul' music.

Martha Reeves

When Martha Reeves was young, she started singing in her grandfather's Pentecostal church. She recorded a record when she was at school, but it wasn't a hit. Later, she worked as a secretary for the Motown record company. One day, a singer didn't arrive for a recording. The studio needed a vocalist and they used Martha. It was the start of a great career: Martha and the Vandellas were very successful, with eight big hits in the '60s.

Nowhere to run

(Chorus)
Nowhere to run to, baby, nowhere to hide.
Got nowhere to run to, baby, nowhere to hide.

It's not love I'm running from.
It's the heartache I (**1**) …… will come,
'Cos I know you're no good for me,
But you've become a part of me.
Everywhere I (**2**) ……, your face I see.
Every step I (**3**) ……, you take with me.

(Repeat chorus)

I know you're no good for me,
But free of you I'll never be, no.
Each night as I sleep,
Into my heart you creep.
I wake up feeling sorry I (**4**) …… you,
Hoping soon that I'll (**5**) …… you.
When I (**6**) …… in the mirror and comb my hair,
I see your face just smiling there.

(Repeat chorus x2)

Glossary
'Cos = Because

5 Work

Have a look!

Find the pages where you:
- interview your partner for a job.
- read about a professional snowboarder.
- play a board game.

Vocabulary

Jobs

1 Listen and repeat. Guess the meaning of the words. Then check your answers.

1 bank manager
2 beauty consultant
3 civil servant
4 computer programmer
5 basketball player
6 bus driver
7 motorbike mechanic
8 construction worker
9 Geography teacher
10 electrical engineer

VOCABULARY PAGE 126, 5.1

2 Look at the hands in photos 1–4. Guess the people's jobs.

Number 1 could be …… .

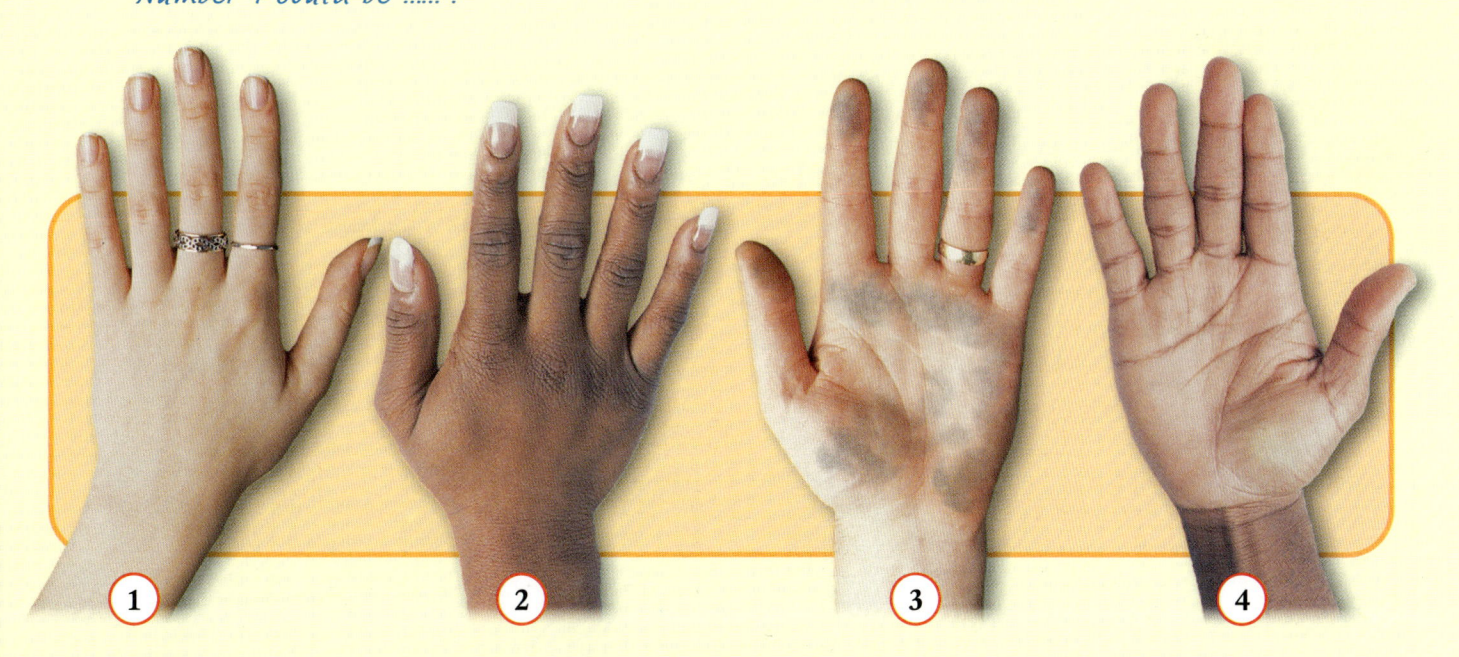

3 Complete the sets of jobs. Use words from exercise 1.

office / hotel / hospital *manager*

1 racing / taxi / train ……
2 French / Maths / Chemistry ……
3 tennis / golf / football ……
4 civil / agricultural / mechanical ……

5a Dream jobs

Reading

1 Look at the photos of DJ Billy B and Cibele Alvarenga. Guess the answers to questions 1–4. Write *Billy*, *Cibele* or *Both*.

1 Which person has had a few accidents?
2 Who has worked in Amsterdam this month?
3 Which person has been to a lot of beautiful places?
4 Who has met a lot of creative people?

2 Read and listen. Then check your answers to exercise 1.

Dream jobs?

Billy B
Club DJ

Can you tell us about your job?
I play in various clubs. I've got a very organized manager, and she finds a lot of work for me. I play about fifteen nights a month, and five of those are usually abroad. This month I've been to Amsterdam and New York City.

What's the best part of your job?
I've travelled a lot recently and I've met a lot of creative people. People annoy me sometimes, because they say that DJing is an easy job. But it's very competitive, and you must be reliable. I know that I'm lucky and I earn a lot of money, but I work hard.

Have you ever had any bad experiences?
Not really, I've never been late for a gig, but I've had a few problems with equipment. The worst thing is if people don't like the music, but that hasn't happened to me.

Do you have any career tips for teenagers?
Listen to the experts on the radio and at clubs. Make a demo tape of your best mixes and send it to some clubs and radio stations. Try to get a job with a small radio station, or buy some equipment and start organizing your own gigs.

Cibele Alvarenga
Professional snowboarder

Can you tell us about your job?
I teach snowboarding, and I've also done photographic sessions for sports magazines. Snowboarding has become really popular and I'm usually very busy. I've also been in a lot of competitions recently. I've even won one or two!

What's the best part of your job?
The best thing is working outdoors in the fresh air. I really love it. I'm only twenty, but I've been to some of the most beautiful places in the world.

Have you ever had any bad experiences?
I'm very competitive and I've had a few accidents! This year I've had two operations on my knee. Some places are scarier than others. I was in the Rockies last year, but I was a bit worried about avalanches.

Do you have any career tips for teenagers?
Well, most of all you must practise and practise. You need to be fit and ambitious. I started late, when I was 17, so don't worry if you start late. There's always time. You can learn the basic skills really quickly.

3 Read the texts again and answer the questions.

1 Does Billy think that his job is easy?
2 Does Billy earn a good salary?
3 Has Billy ever arrived late for a gig?
4 What is the most positive aspect of Cibele's job?
5 What medical problems has Cibele had?
6 Why did Cibele feel scared in the Rockies?

Exploring grammar
Present perfect

The present perfect often refers to experiences in an unfinished time period, for example, *recently, this month, this year.* Never (*ever* in questions) means in your life.

4 Complete the table.
Use *Have, haven't, Has, hasn't, 's, never* and *ever.*

Affirmative		
I / You / We / They	've	travelled a lot recently.
He / She / It	(1)	
Negative		
I / You / We / They	(2)	had any bad experiences.
He / She / It	(3)	
I've (4) ...... been late.		
Questions		
(5) ...... I / you / we / they		had an accident?
(6) ...... he / she / it		
Have you (7) ...... been to New York?		

GRAMMAR ▶ PAGE 120
IRREGULAR VERBS ▶ INSIDE BACK COVER

5 Complete the text. Use the present perfect.

Child labour

It's six o'clock on Sunday evening, and Babu *has been* (be) in the factory all day. He (1) ...... (work) six days this week. Babu's parents sold him to the owners of the factory three months ago, and he (2) ...... (not see) them again this year. Babu and many other children in India (3) ...... (not have) an education.

This isn't only a problem in India. The International Labour Organization (4) ...... (calculate) that 250 million of the world's children are working. The ILO, UNICEF and other organizations (5) ...... (start) to act, but it is a massive problem.

Vocabulary
Adjectives: qualities for jobs

6 Listen and repeat. Guess the meaning of the words. Then check your answers.

1 ambitious   6 fit
2 practical   7 creative
3 experienced   8 organized
4 communicative   9 reliable
5 mature   10 competitive

VOCABULARY ▶ PAGE 126, 5.2

7 Complete the questions. Use the present perfect form of the verbs in the box and *ever.*

> mend   write   arrive   speak   ~~run~~   have

JOBS! JOBS! JOBS! JOBS!

1 Are you fit? *Have you ever run* 3 kilometres? ☐
2 Are you communicative?
...... to a big group of people? ☐
3 Are you creative?
...... an imaginative poem or a story? ☐
4 Are you practical?
...... anything? ☐
5 Are you reliable?
...... late for class or a meeting? ☐
6 Are you experienced?
...... a job before? ☐

Speaking

8 Work in pairs. Ask and answer the questions in exercise 7.

A: *Have you ever run three kilometres?*
B: *No, I haven't.*

Finished?

List the qualities needed for specific jobs.
Athletes must be fit and competitive.

5b The ladder of success

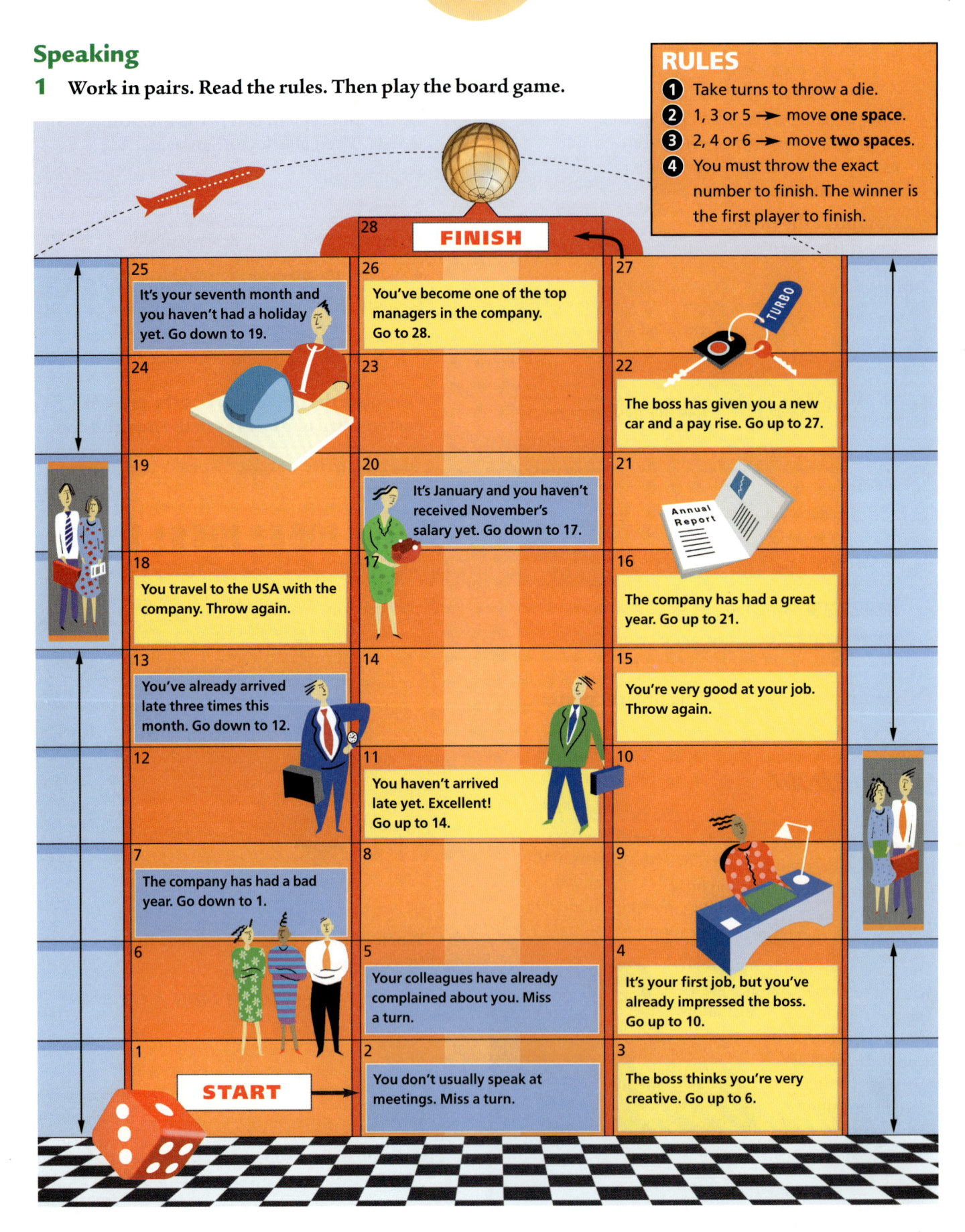

Speaking

1 Work in pairs. Read the rules. Then play the board game.

RULES
1. Take turns to throw a die.
2. 1, 3 or 5 → move **one space**.
3. 2, 4 or 6 → move **two spaces**.
4. You must throw the exact number to finish. The winner is the first player to finish.

28 FINISH

25

26 You've become one of the top managers in the company. Go to 28.

27

24

23

22 The boss has given you a new car and a pay rise. Go up to 27.

19

20 It's January and you haven't received November's salary yet. Go down to 17.

21

18 You travel to the USA with the company. Throw again.

17

16 The company has had a great year. Go up to 21.

13 You've already arrived late three times this month. Go down to 12.

14

15 You're very good at your job. Throw again.

12

11 You haven't arrived late yet. Excellent! Go up to 14.

10

7 The company has had a bad year. Go down to 1.

8

9

6

5 Your colleagues have already complained about you. Miss a turn.

4 It's your first job, but you've already impressed the boss. Go up to 10.

1 **START**

2 You don't usually speak at meetings. Miss a turn.

3 The boss thinks you're very creative. Go up to 6.

25 It's your seventh month and you haven't had a holiday yet. Go down to 19.

Exploring grammar
Present perfect: *yet* and *already*

2 Look at the sentences. Then complete the rules with *yet* and *already*.

1 You've **already** impressed the boss.
2 You haven't had a holiday **yet**.

> **Rules**
> We put (1) ...... at the end of a negative sentence.
> We put (2) ...... before the past participle.

GRAMMAR ➤ PAGE 120

3 Look at the board game again. Find more examples of sentences with *yet* and *already*.

4 Write sentences about Ken and Liz. Use the present perfect and *yet* or *already*.

Ken has already read the job advert.

1 Ken / write / a letter (✔)
2 Liz / get up (✘)
3 Liz / phone / the company (✘)
4 Ken / meet / the interviewer (✔)
5 Ken / accept / the job (✔)
6 Liz / have breakfast (✘)

5 Look at the careers advice and write sentences about you. Use the present perfect and *yet* or *already*.

1 I've already thought about my future.

> **Careers advice**
> 1 Think about your future.
> 2 Study a language.
> 3 Speak to people about different jobs.
> 4 Learn to drive.
> 5 Practise computer skills.
> 6 Think about qualifications.
> 7 Decide on a profession.
> 8 Look at job adverts.

Pronunciation
/h/

6 Listen and repeat.

| 1 have | 3 had | 5 has |
| 2 haven't | 4 holiday | 6 happy |

7 Listen and repeat.

Have you had a happy holiday in the Himalayas?

Speaking

8 In pairs, ask and answer questions about the checklist in exercise 5.

A: *Have you thought about your future yet?*
B: *Yes, I've already thought about it.*

> **Finished?**
>
> Make a list of your top ten jobs.
> *1 – Formula 1 racing driver*

Unit 5 Work 53

5c Interviews

Reading

1 Read the job adverts. Then complete the table.

Job	Qualities
Web page designer	creative, (1) ......
(2)	polite, (3) ......
(4)	experienced
(5)	fit, (6) ......
(7)	responsible, mature, communicative
Trainee mechanic	(8) ......, hard-working

a) Web page designers
We are looking for young people with knowledge of the internet. Our young, dynamic company is offering a fantastic opportunity in our e-commerce department for creative, ambitious people.
£40,000 per annum.
Benefits + car
Contact: Mick@e-books.com

b) New city centre disco
Trance Dance is opening this summer and we need you for our exciting new project! At the moment we have got the following job vacancies:
- Part-time receptionists (must be polite and friendly; knowledge of a foreign language an advantage)
- DJs (experience essential)
- Security guards (for day or night duty; must be fit and reliable)

Please write to
Mr T Adams, Trance Dance

c) Au pair
We are looking for an au pair for our sons Jed, two and Jon, four. We live in Miami Beach, Florida. We will provide a flat and a car for you, and you will accompany the family to our holiday home in the Caribbean. Applicants must be responsible, mature and communicative!
Write to: P.O. Box 23,

d) Wanted
Trainee mechanic required (preferably school-leaver) for motorbike racing team. If you are practical and hard-working we will teach you all that you need to know.
Telephone: 01993 312654

Study skills

Guessing the meaning of words from context

It is often possible to guess the meaning of words from their context. You need to ask the following questions:
- What is the theme of the text?
- Does the word look similar to any words in your language? If yes, is the meaning similar in this text?
- Do you know the meaning of any part of the word?
- What part of speech is the word (noun, adjective, adverb, preposition, etc.)?

2 Find these words in the job adverts. Guess the meanings of the words from their context.

1. offering (advert a)
2. e-commerce (advert a)
3. part-time (advert b)
4. foreign (advert b)
5. provide (advert c)
6. trainee (advert d)
7. school-leaver (advert d)
8. hard-working (advert d)

Writing
A formal letter

3 Compare letters a and b. Write *a* or *b* for sentences 1–5.

1 a

1 We know the name and address of the person who wrote the letter.
2 We know the name and address of the person who receives the letter.
3 We know when the letter was written.
4 The language is more formal.
5 The letter gives more information.

a

6 Church Rd,
OXFORD
OX4 3RT
18th July, 2001

T. Adams
Trance Dance
Manchester
M13 2PJ

Dear Mr Adams,

I am writing about your advert for part-time receptionists. I am 16 years old. I haven't left school yet, but I am taking my exams in June. I have not had any work experience, but I have studied French at school. I think that I am polite and friendly.

Please could you send an application form to the above address? Thank you.

Yours sincerely,
Kevin Grant

b

Dear Manager,

I saw your advert and I can come for an interview if you want. The job sounds OK. I'm a great DJ and I know that I can do it. I'm the person you're looking for. Phone my mobile when you've got a minute: 07979 243672.

Kevin Harte

4 Write a letter asking for an application form. Include this information:
- your address and the date
- the job that you are interested in
- what you have studied
- your experience
- your personal qualities

Listening

5 Listen to the interview. Do you think that the applicant is Kevin Grant or Kevin Harte?

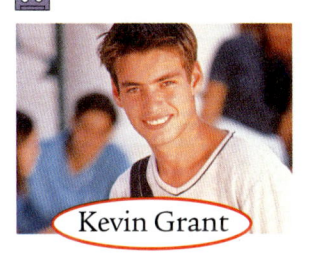

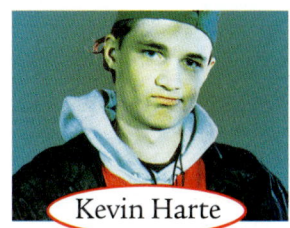

Kevin Grant   Kevin Harte

6 Listen again and write Kevin's answers to these questions.
1 Why do you want to work here?
2 Have you finished school?
3 Have you had any work experience?
4 What can you offer us? What are your personal qualities?
5 Have you got any questions for me?

Speaking

7 Choose a job from the box. Then prepare answers for the questions in exercise 6. In pairs, ask and answer the questions.

computer programmer   DJ   teacher
bank manager   beauty consultant

Finished?

Write about your partner.
Samuel has applied for a job as a DJ.

Progress Check 5

Jobs

1 Put the letters in the correct order.

livic vanters – *civil servant*

1 marmgroper rputomec
2 hoggypare cheater
3 knab ragmane
4 sub derriv
5 crontistoncu krower

Adjectives: qualities for jobs

2 Describe Peter and Pauline. Use the adjectives in the box.

> experienced   reliable   fit
> ambitious   creative   ~~communicative~~

Pauline likes talking to people.
She's communicative.

1 Peter is never late.
2 Pauline wants a better job.
3 Peter has had his job for twenty years.
4 Pauline can write poems.
5 Peter runs 10 kilometres every day.

Present perfect

3 Complete the sentences. Use the present perfect.

Tom *has decided* to improve his image.

1 He …… (find) a job.
2 He …… (start) to get up earlier.
3 He …… (buy) some new clothes.
4 His parents …… (give) him a car.
5 He …… (change) his hairstyle.
6 He and his girlfriend …… (save) £900.

Tom before   Tom now

4 Complete the sentences. Use the present perfect.

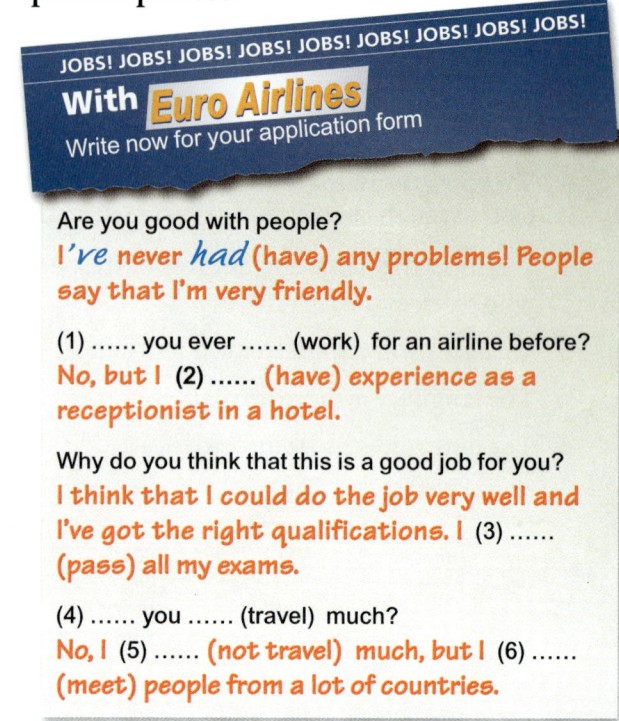

JOBS! JOBS! JOBS! JOBS! JOBS! JOBS! JOBS! JOBS!
With Euro Airlines
Write now for your application form

Are you good with people?
I've never **had** (have) any problems! People say that I'm very friendly.

(1) …… you ever …… (work) for an airline before?
No, but I (2) …… (have) experience as a receptionist in a hotel.

Why do you think that this is a good job for you?
I think that I could do the job very well and I've got the right qualifications. I (3) …… (pass) all my exams.

(4) …… you …… (travel) much?
No, I (5) …… (not travel) much, but I (6) …… (meet) people from a lot of countries.

Present perfect: *yet* and *already*

5 Look at Cibele's checklist. Write sentences with the present perfect and *yet* or *already*.

1 She's already spoken to her manager.

Competition-Checklist
1 Speak to my manager. ✓
2 Phone the travel agent ✗
3 Read the competition rules. ✓
4 Check the equipment. ✓
5 Look for my passport! ✗
6 Buy a camera. ✗

6 Extreme

Have a look!
Find the pages where you:
- read about Everest.
- speak about dangerous situations.
- listen to an interview with a skysurfer.

Vocabulary
Sports

1 Listen and repeat the words in the box. Which sports are not in the pictures?

> parachuting   climbing   skiing   diving   canoeing   sailing
> skating   surfing   snowboarding   skateboarding

2 Complete the table. Use the words from exercise 1. **VOCABULARY** PAGE 126, 6.1

Water sports	Mountain sports	Street sports	Other sports
			parachuting

Speaking

3 Work in pairs. Ask and answer questions about the sports.

Have you ever tried …?
Would you like to try …?
Are you interested in …?

57

6a The summit

Reading

1 Complete the text with the numbers in the box. Then listen and check.

> 8,848   1924   ~~250~~   65,000   1978   1,000

2 Read the text again. Are the sentences true or false?

1. Everybody must use oxygen cylinders when they climb Everest.
2. People die in the 'Death Zone' because it is very cold.
3. There are expeditions to Everest every year.
4. It is impossible to climb Everest alone.
5. Mallory was the first person to reach the summit of Everest.
6. About 1,000 people have died on Everest.

Exploring grammar

Present perfect and past simple

3 Underline the time expressions in examples a–d. What tense do we use
- when the time period is finished?
- when the time period is unfinished?

Examples

a. I have <u>never</u> been so tired <u>in my life</u>.
b. In the past 50 years, more than 1,000 people have climbed Everest.
c. Mallory died on the mountain in 1924.
d. In 1980 Messner reached the summit alone.

GRAMMAR PAGE 120

The summit

Mount Everest got its name from the surname of the British engineer and surveyor, Sir George Everest, but in Nepali the name of the mountain is Sagarmatha, meaning 'Goddess Mother of the World'. It is a beautiful but dangerous place. In winter there are sometimes winds of *250* kilometres per hour and temperatures of –60° C. The (**1**) .... metre summit is the highest place on Earth. At that altitude, it is difficult to survive.

Climbers say that the 'Death Zone' starts at 7,900 metres. Here the human body starts to die because there isn't enough oxygen, but people can survive for a short time. After each step a climber must stop and try desperately to breathe. In (**2**) ...., Reinhold Messner and Peter Habeler became the first people to climb Everest without oxygen cylinders. In 1980 Messner reached the summit alone. Messner said, 'I was in continual agony. I have never been so tired in my life.'

So why climb Everest? 'Because it's there,' said climber George Mallory, before he died on the mountain in (**3**) .... Many climbers tried to conquer Everest before Tenzing Norgay and Edmund Hillary finally reached the summit in 1953. In the past 50 years, more than (**4**) .... people have climbed Everest and more than 150 have died. Most of the bodies are still on the mountain, because it is too difficult to find or move them.

Every year more people want to climb the world's highest mountain. If you are fit and you have (**5**) .... dollars, you can train and then climb the mountain with professionals. But as more people try to reach the summit, there are more accidents. The price of climbing Everest is high, and some people pay with their lives.

6a

4 Choose the correct form of the verbs.

> **Everest records**
>
> Some people **climbed** / **have climbed** Everest more than once in their lives.
>
> 1 Appa Sherpa **climbed** / **has climbed** the mountain eleven times so far.
> 2 He first **climbed** / **has climbed** the mountain in 1983.
> 3 Junko Tabei **became** / **has become** the first woman on the summit in 1975.
> 4 Temba Tsheri **was** / **has been** 15 when he reached the summit in 2001.
> 5 Sherman Bull **reached** / **has reached** the summit when he was 64.
> 6 Avalanches **caused** / **have caused** most deaths on Everest.

5 Complete the dialogue with the correct form of the past simple and the present perfect.

Baz: *Have you ever tried* (ever try) surfing?
Sue: No, but I (**1**) …… (climb) a lot.
Baz: Really? I (**2**) …… (never try) climbing. When (**3**) …… you …… (start)?
Sue: I (**4**) …… (start) two years ago. This year I (**5**) …… (have) three climbing holidays.
Baz: Where (**6**) …… you …… (go) last month?
Sue: Last month I (**7**) …… (go) to Bermuda.
Baz: But there aren't any mountains there.
Sue: I know, so I (**8**) …… (stay) on the beach!

Pronunciation

Recognizing contractions

6 Listen and repeat.

1 You've started surfing.   3 She's tried skiing.
2 You started surfing.   4 She tried skiing.

7 Listen and write the five sentences.

Speaking

8 Work in pairs. Ask and answer questions about experiences. Use the present perfect and the past simple.

> A: Have you ever been in a canoe?
> B: Yes, I have.
> A: Where were you?
> B: In the USA.
> A: Was it good?

1 …… (try) skiing?
2 …… (see) people windsurfing?
3 …… (try) skating?
4 …… (go) to a football match?
5 …… (walk) in the mountains?

> **Finished?**
>
> Write about your experiences of different sports.
> *I've never tried skiing.*
> *I've played football a lot. I first played in a team when I was eleven.*

Unit 6 *Extreme*

6b Skysurfers

Vocabulary

Sports equipment

1 Check the meaning of the words in the box. Then match the words with pictures 1–10.

> oxygen cylinder   helmet   bodyboard
> skateboard   surfboard   goggles   skates
> wetsuit   parachute   mask

1 bodyboard

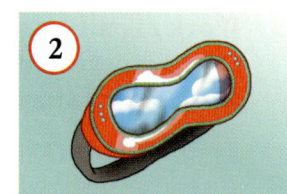

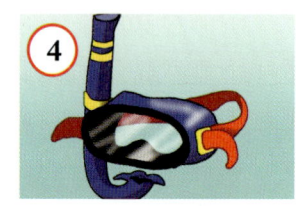

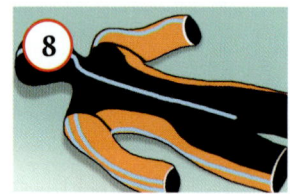

2 Write sentences about sports equipment.

You need goggles for skiing.

1 diving
2 canoeing
3 roller skating
4 surfing

VOCABULARY   PAGE 126, 6.2

Listening

3 Listen to an interview with Carl King, a skysurfer. Which topics do Carl and the reporter mention?

a price
b equipment
c countries
d dangers
e history of the sport
f advice to beginners

4 Choose a or b to complete each sentence. Then listen to the interview again and check your answers.

SKYSURF QUIZ

1 A skysurfer can travel at …
   a 180 kilometres per hour.
   b 280 kilometres per hour.

2 People first jumped with boards in …
   a 1980.   b 1992.

3 The original name of the sport was …
   a surf-jumping.   b air-surfing.

4 The first competitions were in …
   a 1987.   b 1992.

5 Skysurfers are usually experienced …
   a surfers.   b skydivers.

6 Clubs are the best places to learn skysurfing because you can …
   a use their equipment.   b meet champions.

Exploring grammar
Present perfect: *for* and *since*

5 Complete the table with examples 1–5. When do we use *since* and *for*?

This tells us when an activity started.	This tells us the duration of an activity.
1	

1 People have jumped with boards since 1980.
2 Things didn't really change for seven years.
3 It's been a popular sport since 1992.
4 I've been interested in parachuting since I was sixteen.
5 I've had my board for two years now.

GRAMMAR PAGE 120

6 Complete the sentences with *for* or *since*.

Skates
Skating has been popular *for* years, but things have changed a lot (**1**) …… 1760 when people first wore skates.
Inline skates have existed (**2**) …… 1819. A Frenchman called Petibledin invented them, but they didn't become popular (**3**) …… 170 years.
Skateboards have existed (**4**) …… more than 40 years. Surfers invented them because they wanted to surf on the street. Skateboards were unpopular (**5**) …… a time at the end of the 1980s, but they're big again now.

7 Complete the sentences with the present perfect and *for* or *since*.

Zoe *has been* (be) a snowboarding fan *for* years.

1 She …… (be) in a new club …… six weeks.
2 She …… (have) these goggles …… last January.
3 She …… (use) the same board …… 1999.
4 She …… (not wear) skis …… two years.
5 She …… (win) six trophies …… she started.

Present perfect: *just*

8 Look at the examples and choose the correct word to complete the rule.

Dave **has just jumped** from the plane.
We**'ve just seen** an incredible jump.

We use **just** + present perfect a **short** / **long** time after an action.

GRAMMAR PAGE 121

9 Look at pictures 1–4. Write sentences with the present perfect and *just*.

She*'s just invented* (invent) a new sport.

1 He …… (see) Santa Claus. 
2 She …… (climb) a mountain. 
3 They …… (start) a game. 
4 The game …… (finish).

10 Complete the sentences with your ideas. Use the present perfect and *just*.

I'm tired. I've just finished a game of basketball.

1 I'm tired.
2 I'm really happy.
3 My friend is angry.
4 We're scared.

Finished?
Invent a new sport and explain it.
Skateball is my new sport. You need …

Unit 6 *Extreme*

6c Risk

Reading

1 Read the quiz. Choose answer a or b for each situation.

The risk test

Some sports are dangerous, but how can you avoid the risks? Try the risk test and find out.

1 Some of your friends are experienced walkers. They've invited you to go walking in the mountains for a day. The weather has been excellent for days. What must you take?
   a A map and compass.
   b Extra food and extra clothes.

2 You have just bought a new surfboard and you are going to drive to the beach. What must you do before you leave home?
   a Put on your wetsuit.
   b Tell another person where you are going.

3 You are diving and you are 25 metres underwater. You've got a problem with your oxygen cylinder and you can't breathe. What do you do?
   a Go immediately to the boat.
   b Stay where you are and share oxygen with another diver. Then go to the boat with the other diver.

4 Your friend has just had an accident because he couldn't control his skateboard. He is on the road and he can't move. What should you do?
   a Don't move him. Make signals to traffic and wait for help.
   b Move him from the road immediately.

5 You're surfing in Australia, but you've heard that there's sometimes a danger from sharks. How can you enjoy your sport and avoid danger?
   a Surf with other people and don't surf in the evening.
   b Don't surf with other people and don't surf at midday.

6 You want to go snowboarding, but you've heard that there's a risk of avalanches in the area. What do you do?
   a Go snowboarding but be very quiet. Noises can cause avalanches.
   b Don't go snowboarding today.

Speaking

2 Work in pairs. Compare your answers. Use some of these expressions.

- What answer did you choose?
- I agree, because …
- I disagree, because …
- Maybe you're right.

Listening

3 Listen to a team of survival experts and check your answers to exercise 1.

4 Answer the questions. Then listen again and check.

1 Why is the weather a problem in the mountains?
2 Where can you put on your wetsuit?
3 Do people always dive in pairs?
4 What must you wait for in situation 4?
5 When are sharks most active?
6 Do noises usually cause avalanches?

Writing
Presenting factual information

SPORTS FACTFILE:
surfing

1. Surfing is becoming the world's most popular water sport. It's exciting and fun for people of all ages. All you need is a surfboard, a wetsuit and a lot of enthusiasm.

2. Surfing started a long time ago. In the 18th century, explorers sailing around islands in the Pacific saw people surfing the waves on wooden boards.

3. These days, equipment can be expensive, but it's possible to hire boards and wetsuits from surf schools or shops. You can also buy second-hand equipment – a good idea because it can be expensive.

4. Safety is important. The sea can be dangerous so it's a good idea to surf with other people, and to avoid places with rocks.

5. Practice makes perfect! Start with some lessons at a surf school and maybe one day you'll surf some of the three-metre waves in Hawaii or Mexico. I'm not very good yet, but I only started three months ago.

5 Read the factfile and answer the questions.
1. How old is the sport of surfing?
2. What equipment do you need for surfing?
3. Where can you find some of the biggest waves?

6 Complete the checklist with the words in the box.

> Check   Plan   repeat   interesting
> boring   information   introduction

7 Read the factfile again. Answer the questions.
1. Does the text start with an introduction?
2. Are there any interesting facts in the text?
3. What information does the writer repeat in paragraph 3?
4. What is the personal information in paragraph 5?

8 Find out about a sport and write a factfile. Use the checklist from exercise 6 and include this information.
- a general description of the sport
- when, where and how it started
- what equipment people use now
- safety
- where / how to learn

Writing checklist: presenting facts
☺ 1 *Plan* your work.
   2 Find some …… facts.
   3 Always start with an …… .
   4 …… your work when you finish and correct any mistakes.
☹ 5 Don't …… information.
   6 Don't include …… information.
   7 Don't include personal …… .

Finished?
Exchange factfiles with a partner. Use the checklist from exercise 6 to evaluate your partner's text.

Unit 6 *Extreme* **63**

Progress Check 6

Sports

1 Match the words in the box with pictures 1–6. Then write the names of the sports.

> canoeist   diver   climber   skater
> surfer   parachutist

1 climber – climbing

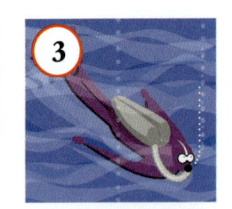

Sports equipment

2 Read the definitions and write the names of the equipment.

1 This protects your head.
2 You can breathe under the water with this.
3 You stand on this when you're skateboarding.
4 You need this when you jump from a plane.
5 This protects your face under the water.
6 You can travel on the water in this.

Present perfect and past simple

3 Write sentences with the correct form of the verbs. Use the present perfect or the past simple.

1 She …… (win) three trophies this year.
2 She …… (win) her first trophy when she was sixteen.
3 She …… (visit) Canada this year.
4 She …… (go) to Italy and Switzerland last year.
5 She …… (travel) 12,000 kilometres in the last eight days.
6 She …… (be) twenty three weeks ago.

for and *since*

4 Complete the sentences with *for* or *since*.

1 Beach volleyball has been an Olympic sport …… 1996.
2 In a game of beach volleyball, people play …… about twenty minutes.
3 People have surfed …… hundreds of years.
4 In 1993 Gary Frick travelled …… 131 days on a jetski.
5 Stephan van den Berg has been the world windsurfing champion five times …… 1979.

Present perfect: *just*

5 Write sentences. Use the present perfect and *just*.

He …… (win) a race.

He's just won a race.

1 They …… (have) an accident.
2 He …… (see) a shark.
3 She …… (buy) some new skates.
4 They …… (lose) the match.
5 Her parachute …… (open).

64

The World of English 3

North Street (pages 66 and 67)

Revision: present perfect
Function: Making suggestions

1. Has Maxine had problems with Matt Gray?

Culture File (pages 68 and 69)

Topic: Teenage problems

2. Who wrote the poem about bullying?

The Story of Pop (page 70)

Artist: The Beatles
Type of music: Merseybeat
Song: Can't buy me love

3. What's the name of the river in Liverpool?

North Street

A few problems

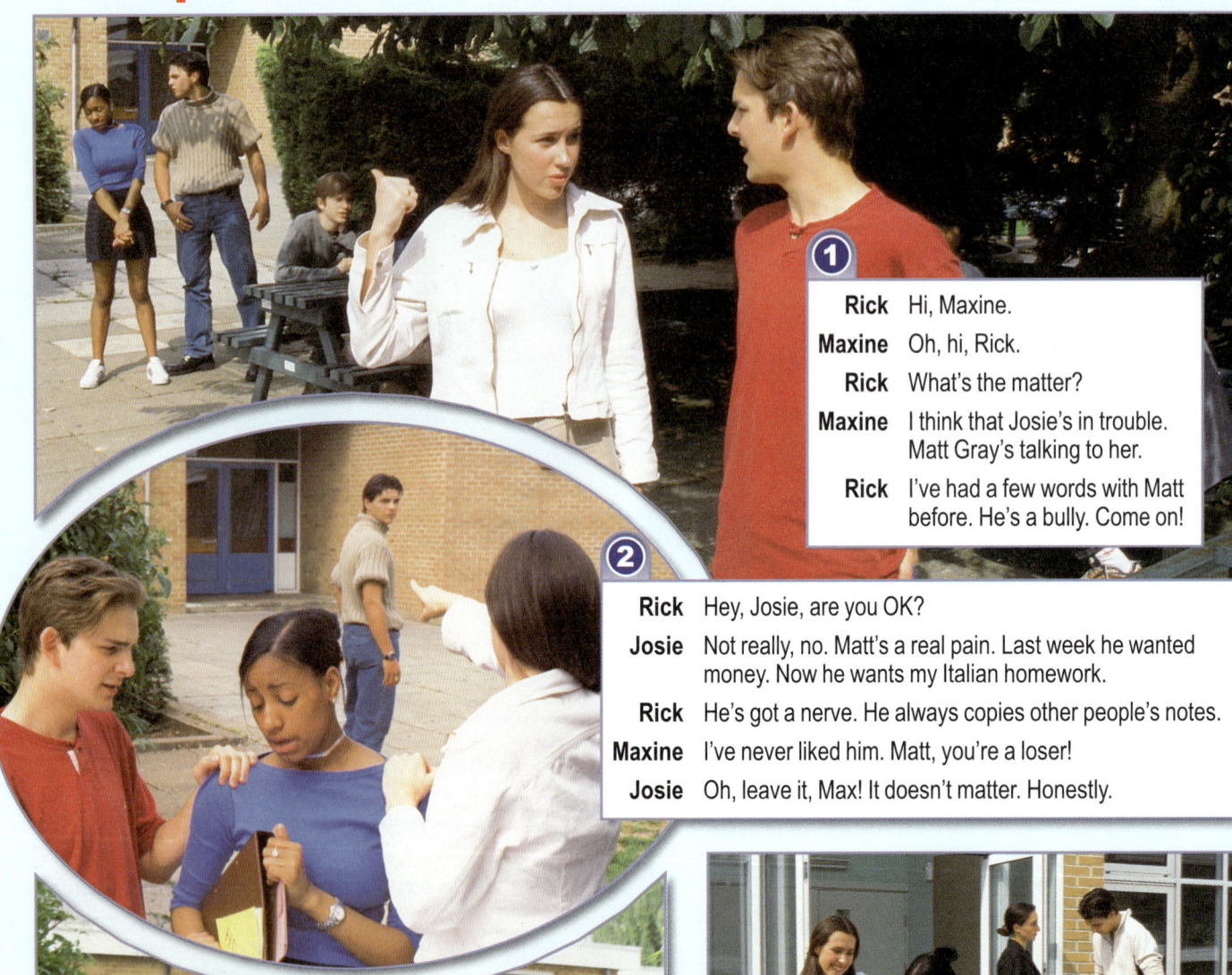

1

Rick   Hi, Maxine.
Maxine   Oh, hi, Rick.
Rick   What's the matter?
Maxine   I think that Josie's in trouble. Matt Gray's talking to her.
Rick   I've had a few words with Matt before. He's a bully. Come on!

2

Rick   Hey, Josie, are you OK?
Josie   Not really, no. Matt's a real pain. Last week he wanted money. Now he wants my Italian homework.
Rick   He's got a nerve. He always copies other people's notes.
Maxine   I've never liked him. Matt, you're a loser!
Josie   Oh, leave it, Max! It doesn't matter. Honestly.

3

Rick   Now, come on, Josie. What are you going to do?
Maxine   Why don't you talk to someone?
Josie   I suppose so.
Rick   You should definitely find a way to stop him.
Josie   Yes, you're right.

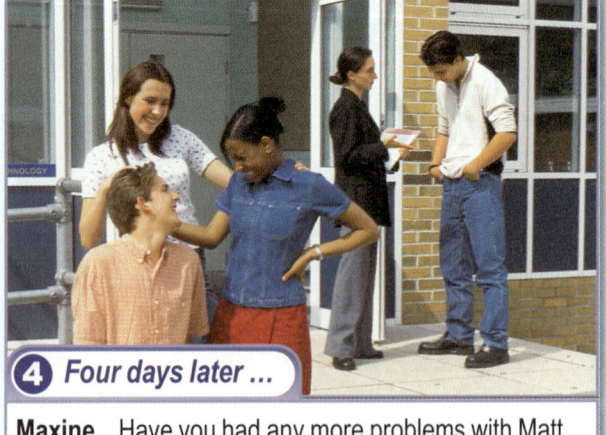

4 Four days later ...

Maxine   Have you had any more problems with Matt since the other day?
Josie   No, I haven't. But he's having a few problems with Ms Rossi!
Rick   I can't believe it – he had your Italian notes for four days but he failed the exam.
Josie   Yes, poor Matt. I gave him last year's notes!
Maxine   Ha, ha! Nice one, Josie!

Reading

1 Read and listen to North Street. Then answer the questions.

1. Why was Maxine worried about Josie?
2. Has Josie had problems with Matt before?
3. What did Matt want from Josie this time?
4. What did Maxine suggest to Josie?
5. Why did Matt fail the Italian exam?

Useful expressions

2 Find the expressions in the story. Then check their meaning.

1. Matt's a real pain.
2. He's got a nerve.
3. It doesn't matter.
4. Nice one, Josie!

Dialogue

Making suggestions

3 Look at this extract from North Street. Listen and repeat. Concentrate on your rhythm and intonation.

A: Now, come on, *Josie*. What are you going to do?
B: Why don't you *talk to someone*?
C: I suppose so.
A: You should definitely *find a way to stop him*.
C: Yes, you're right.

4 Think of solutions for these problems.

1. a friend is always late for school

   1 ask your parents to wake you up
   2 buy a new alarm clock

2. a friend wants to be fitter
3. a friend is a computer addict
4. a friend needs some money

5 In groups of three, discuss the problems in exercise 4. Use exercise 3 as a model. Substitute the blue words to form your own dialogues.

A: *Now, come on, Sandra. What are you going to do?*
B: *Why don't you ask your parents to wake you up?*
C: *I suppose so.*
A: *You should definitely buy a new alarm clock.*
C: *Yes, you're right.*

The World of English 3 **67**

Culture File 3

Teenage problems

1 Read the poem. What problem has the person got? Think of a title for the poem.

> There are people here but I feel alone.
> There are people here but they don't see
> How cruel words are hurting me.
> I try to be strong.
> I'm not wrong.
> It's not my fault,
> But who can I speak to?
> Who can I phone?
> I feel so alone.

2 Read the poem again and then read the text. Answer the questions.
1. Did people know about Kath's problem when she wrote the poem?
2. Where did Kath have problems with the bullies?
3. How do people contact ChildLine?
4. When can people contact the trained volunteers at ChildLine?
5. Who helped Kath with her problems?

3 What seven types of problem does the text mention? How do you say the words in your language?

A sixteen-year-old girl called Kath wrote this poem in her diary. She had problems with bullies at school. They insulted her every day because of her race and colour. Her life became very difficult.

But how many teenagers have this type of problem? In Britain an organization called ChildLine started in 1986 to give confidential telephone help to young people. People can phone ChildLine 24 hours a day, seven days a week, and talk to a trained volunteer about their problems. ChildLine has helped more than one million young people with their problems. A lot of the calls were about bullies, but people had a lot of other problems, for example: family relationships, eating problems, exam stress, worries about friends, depression and racism.

And Kath? She talked to ChildLine and then to her parents and teachers. They helped her to solve her problems and now she's much happier. Adolescence can be a difficult time, and the statistics show that a lot of people need advice. So remember, if you've got a problem, don't wait too long – speak to someone soon.

4 Look at pictures 1–5. Do you think any of these things are necessary in a school? Why / why not?

1 Security guard and metal detector
2 Surveillance camera
3 Student ID card
4 Sniffer dog
5 Police patrol

5 Listen to an interview with the principal of a high school in Los Angeles. Which things in exercise 4 does he have in his school?

6 Listen again and choose the correct answer.

1 **Some** / **All** schools in Los Angeles have metal detectors.
2 **Some** / **All** schools in Los Angeles have had police patrols.
3 The students feel **unhappy** / **safer** because of the security.
4 There **is** / **isn't** strict security in all American schools.
5 There are now **fewer** / **more** problems with guns and violence.
6 There **is** / **isn't** a drug problem at this principal's school.

Project

Imagine you have a problem with something at school. Use the ideas below or think of your own.

- You've just moved to the school. You don't know anyone and you feel very lonely.
- You've got important exams next month. You haven't started revising yet and you're very worried.
- You've lost some money at school. You think someone stole it when you were in the playground.

Write a paragraph describing what's happened and how you're feeling. Exchange paragraphs with another group and read the problems. Write back suggesting things that they / the school should do.

The World of English 3

The Story of Pop 3

Merseybeat

1 Read and listen. Then answer the questions.

1. What musical styles did British bands adapt?
2. Where did the name 'Merseybeat' come from?
3. In which city did The Beatles start?
4. Why were the first Beatles hits so popular?
5. What adjectives describe their later music?

2 Read the song and write *True* or *False*. Then listen and check.

1. The singer will buy anything for his friend.
2. The singer thinks that money is important.
3. The singer thinks that he can use money to buy love.
4. The singer bought a lot of presents for his friend.
5. The singer hasn't got much money.

Merseybeat

In the 1950s and 1960s, rhythm and blues, and rock and roll, became popular in Europe. In Britain, bands adapted these styles to create a new sound with a very distinctive rhythm, or 'beat'.

An important centre of British 'beat' music was Liverpool, a city on the River Mersey, in the north of England. A lot of new bands started in Liverpool, and their exciting, fresh style was called 'Merseybeat'.

The Beatles

The Beatles were the biggest Merseybeat band of the '60s. Their first hits were simple but irresistible, and they had millions of fans. Later, their music became more serious and sophisticated, and they influenced thousands of other bands. The Beatles became the most successful band in the history of pop music, and their music is still very popular today.

Can't buy me love

Can't buy me love, love
Can't buy me love.
I'll buy you a diamond ring my friend if it makes you feel alright.
I'll get you anything my friend if it makes you feel alright.
'Cos I don't care too much for money, money can't buy me love.

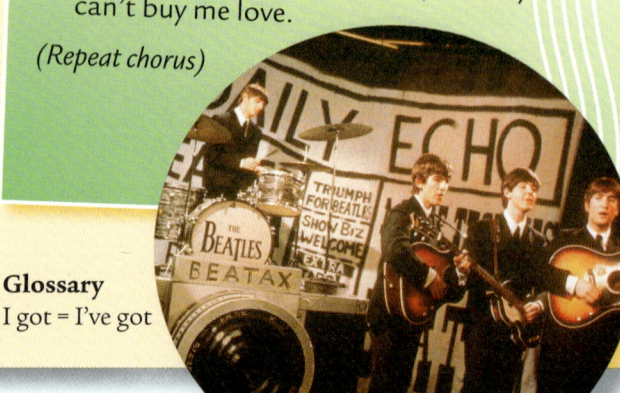

I'll give you all I got to give if you say you love me too.
I may not have a lot to give but what I got I'll give to you.
I don't care too much for money, money can't buy me love.

(Chorus)
Can't buy me love, everybody tells me so
Can't buy me love, no, no, no, no.
Say you don't need no diamond rings and I'll be satisfied.
Tell me that you want the kind of things that money just can't buy.
I don't care too much for money, money can't buy me love.

(Repeat chorus)

Glossary
I got = I've got

7 Microchip magic

Have a look!
Find the pages where you:
- write a description of a website.
- listen to people talking about the future.
- read about how to play a computer game.

Vocabulary
Computers

1 Match the words in the box with pictures 1–10. Then listen and check.

> joystick   keyboard   monitor   mouse
> mouse mat   printer   scanner   screen
> speaker   webcam

1 scanner

VOCABULARY PAGE 127, 7.1

Pronunciation
The alphabet: revision

2 Listen and repeat. Can you guess what the abbreviations mean?

1 CD   2 PC   3 WWW   4 DVD   5 HD

Speaking

3 Spell the words from exercise 1. Test your partner.

A: How do you spell 'scanner'?
B: S – C – A ...

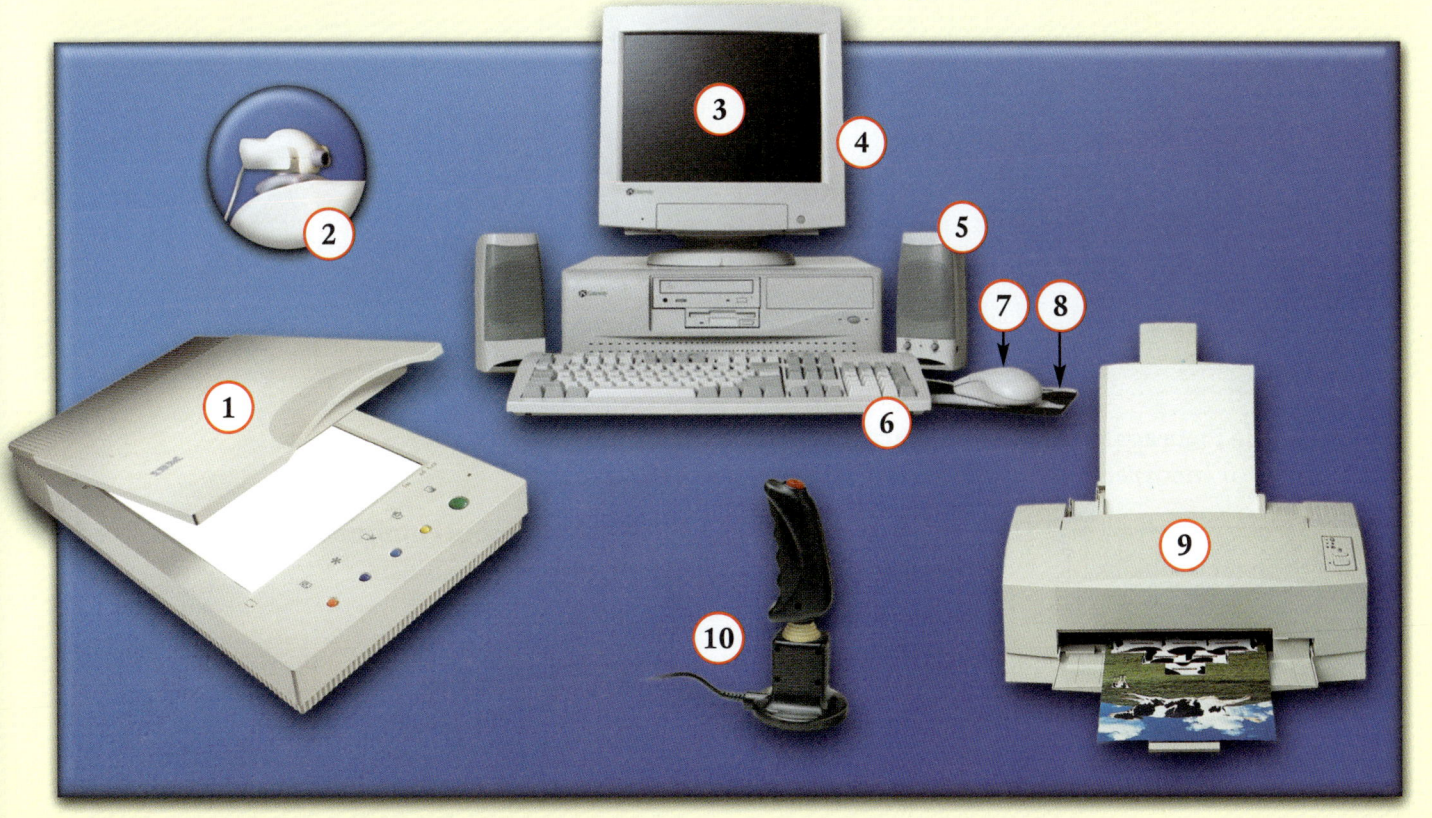

71

7a Game over

Reading

1 Read and listen. Then match texts 1–4 with pictures a–d.

Screen 1 – d

Castle Master Hints for Level 1

Castle Master, troll, guard, torch, ring, cup, key

swim, jump, walk, run, climb, pick up

Screen 1 > The red river
Climb down the ladder. Go slowly or you might fall into the red river. Don't swim across the river – you won't survive! Jump on the blocks, but don't stop on any black blocks. If you stop on a black block for two seconds, you'll lose a life.

Screen 2 > The tunnel
Walk through the tunnel and pick up the diamond rings. They'll give you extra energy. Remember to pick up the torch at the beginning of the tunnel, or you might not see the door to the trophy room.

Screen 3 > The trophy room
In the trophy room you must drink from a magic cup. If you don't drink from it, you'll lose energy. Take the green cup and you'll see the question, 'Is this the magic cup?' If you answer 'Yes', and you drink from the cup, you'll become invisible for ten seconds. Open the white door and quickly go through into the magic chamber.

Screen 4 > The magic chamber
There's always a guard in here and you might see a troll. If the guard sees you, you'll die; but if you're still invisible, you'll be OK. Run across the chamber and pick up the gold key. If you've got the key, a door will open. Go through the door and you've completed level 1!

2 Read the texts again. Are the instructions correct or incorrect?

    Don't swim across the river. *Correct.*

1. Stop on the black blocks in the river.
2. Use a torch in the tunnel.
3. Drink from the yellow cup in the trophy room.
4. Don't go through the white door into the magic chamber.
5. Pick up the gold key in the magic chamber.

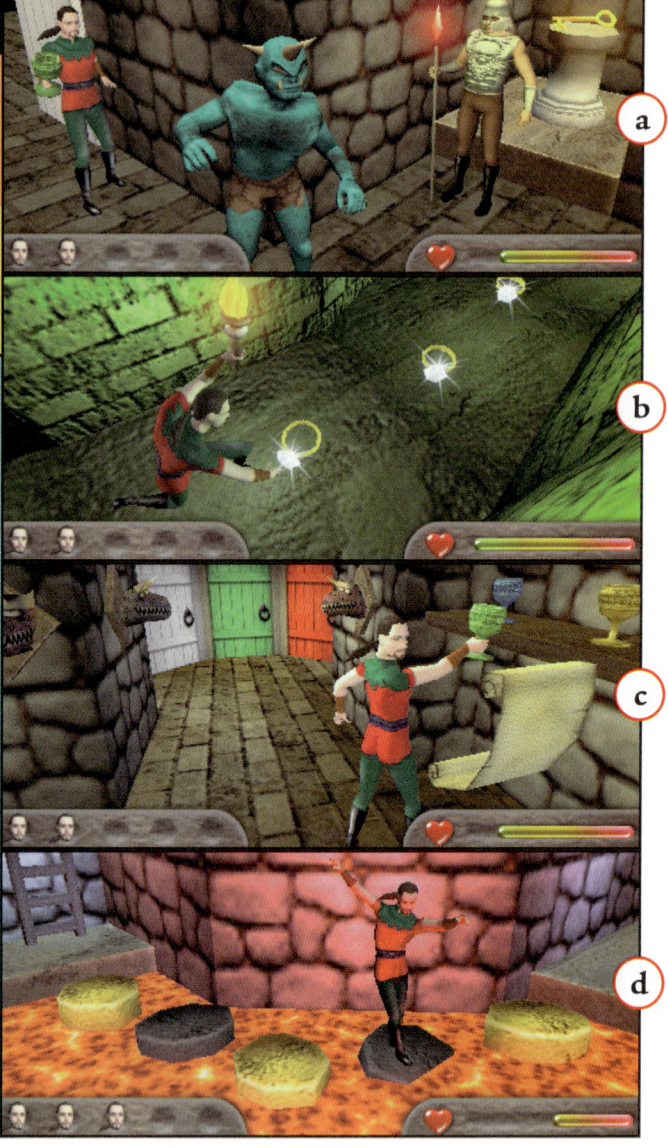

Vocabulary

Movement: verbs + prepositions

3 Find five more combinations of these words in exercise 1.

1 climb down

Verbs	Prepositions
climb go jump run swim walk	across down on through

VOCABULARY PAGE 127, 7.2

Exploring grammar
will and *might*

4 Read the rules and examples. Then complete the table.

Rules
We use **will** and **won't** + infinitive to express certainty. **You'll see** the question. **You won't survive**.
We use **might** and **might not** + infinitive to express possibility. Go slowly or you **might fall**. You **might not see** the door.

	Affirmative	Negative
Certainty	will	(1) ……
Possibility	(2) ……	(3) ……

GRAMMAR ➤ PAGE 121

5 What is your opinion? Complete the sentences with *will*, *won't*, *might* and *might not*.

People *might* have robots as pets.

1. Computers …… be faster in the future.
2. Italy …… win the next football World Cup.
3. Humans …… become extinct.
4. Money …… exist in the future.
5. A person from this class …… become President.

6 Write sentences about the future. Use *will*, *won't*, *might* or *might not* and the words from the table.

I	play football	soon.
My friend	finish this book	today.
We	live in France	this week.
	buy a motorbike	this year.
	be rich	in ten years.

I might play football this week.
My friend won't buy a motorbike this year.

First conditional

We use the first conditional to talk about the probable consequence of an action.

7 Look at the table and complete the rule with *infinitive* and *present simple*.

Action	Consequence
If the guard **sees** you,	you'll **die**.
If you **swim** across the river,	you **won't survive**.
If you **don't drink**,	you'll **lose** energy
Rule	
If + (1) ……, +	will / won't + (2) ……

GRAMMAR ➤ PAGE 121

8 Complete the sentences. Use the first conditional.

If I pass my exams, I'll buy a computer.

1. buy a computer / study at home
2. study at home / not see my friends
3. not see my friends / go crazy
4. go crazy / not pass my exams
5. not pass my exams / not find a job
6. not find a job / sell the computer

9 Look at the pictures and invent rules for Level 2 of Castle Master. Use the first conditional.

If you pick up the sword, you'll have special powers.

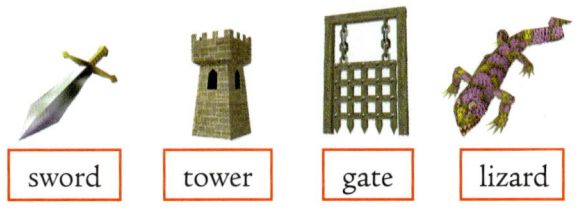

sword | tower | gate | lizard

Finished?
Write about a computer game that you know.
My favourite game is Gran Turismo 3.

7b Virtual world

Listening

1 Look at the magazine cover and listen. Which articles do Lucy and Mark mention?

2 Listen again. Who has these opinions: Lucy or Mark?

1 Lucy

1 *Virtual World* is a good magazine.
2 Virtual schools are a good idea.
3 You can't talk to a computer.
4 Schools might not exist in the future.
5 Real schools are more interesting than virtual schools.

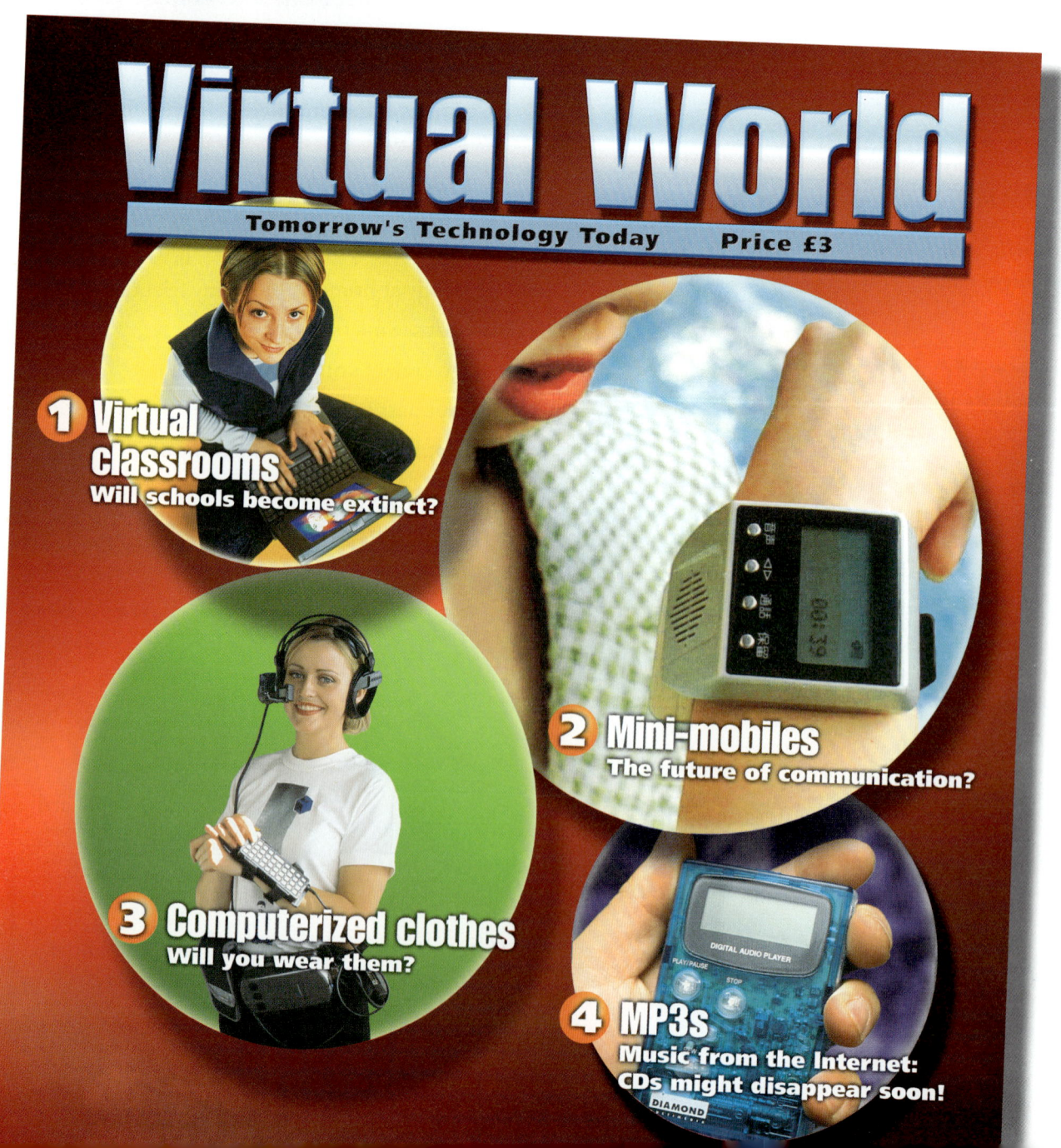

Virtual World
Tomorrow's Technology Today — Price £3

1 Virtual classrooms
Will schools become extinct?

2 Mini-mobiles
The future of communication?

3 Computerized clothes
Will you wear them?

4 MP3s
Music from the Internet: CDs might disappear soon!

Exploring grammar
Second conditional

We use the second conditional to talk about improbable or hypothetical situations.

3 Look at these opinions. Do you agree or disagree?

1. If your school closed, you wouldn't see your friends.
2. If students used a computer all day, they'd be bored.
3. You wouldn't study much if you didn't have a teacher.
4. If it was possible to choose, most students would stay at home.

4 Look again at the sentences in exercise 3. Then complete the rule with a, b or c.

Rule
We form the second conditional with ……
a **If** + **past simple** and **would** + **infinitive**.
b **If** + **would** and **past simple** + **infinitive**.
c **If** + **will** and **would** + **past simple**.

GRAMMAR ▶ PAGE 121

5 Complete the sentences with the words in the box.

be ~~didn't~~ wasn't had didn't have wouldn't

If computers *didn't* exist, life would be more difficult.

1. If school …… obligatory, I wouldn't go.
2. If teachers were robots, classes …… be fun.
3. People would be bored if they …… have mobile phones.
4. I wouldn't …… healthy if I used a computer all day.
5. If we didn't …… schools, people would still study.
6. If I …… a robot, it would do my homework.

6 Complete the sentences with your ideas. Use the second conditional.

If computer games were cheaper, *I'd buy them more often*.

1. If I had a lot of money, ……
2. I'd study more if ……
3. If I didn't go to school, ……
4. My parents would be surprised if ……
5. Life would be great if ……

Speaking

7 Work in pairs. Read and compare your opinions from exercise 6.

Vocabulary
The internet

8 Match sentence halves 1–8 and a–h.

Internet quiz Test your 'cyberspeak'.

1. When you are *online* …
2. When you *download* information …
3. *Chat rooms* are …
4. *Search engines* help you …
5. *Viruses* can cause …
6. A *website* is a place …
7. *E-mail* is a way of …
8. *Cyberpals* are …

a … with information on the internet.
b … to find websites.
c … sending messages on the internet.
d … you transfer it from the internet to your computer.
e … places to talk on the internet.
f … friends you talk to on the internet.
g … you are connected to the internet.
h … problems with your computer.

VOCABULARY ▶ PAGE 127, 7.3

Finished?

Write about how you use the internet.
I don't spend much time online.

7c Websites

Reading

1 Read and listen. If you had a computer here, which of the websites would you visit? Give each website 1, 2, 3 or 4 points.

National Geographic – 1

1 very interesting
2 quite interesting
3 not very interesting
4 really boring

2 Read the text again. On which websites would you find these things?

1 a magazine
2 reviews
3 a sports section
4 MP3s

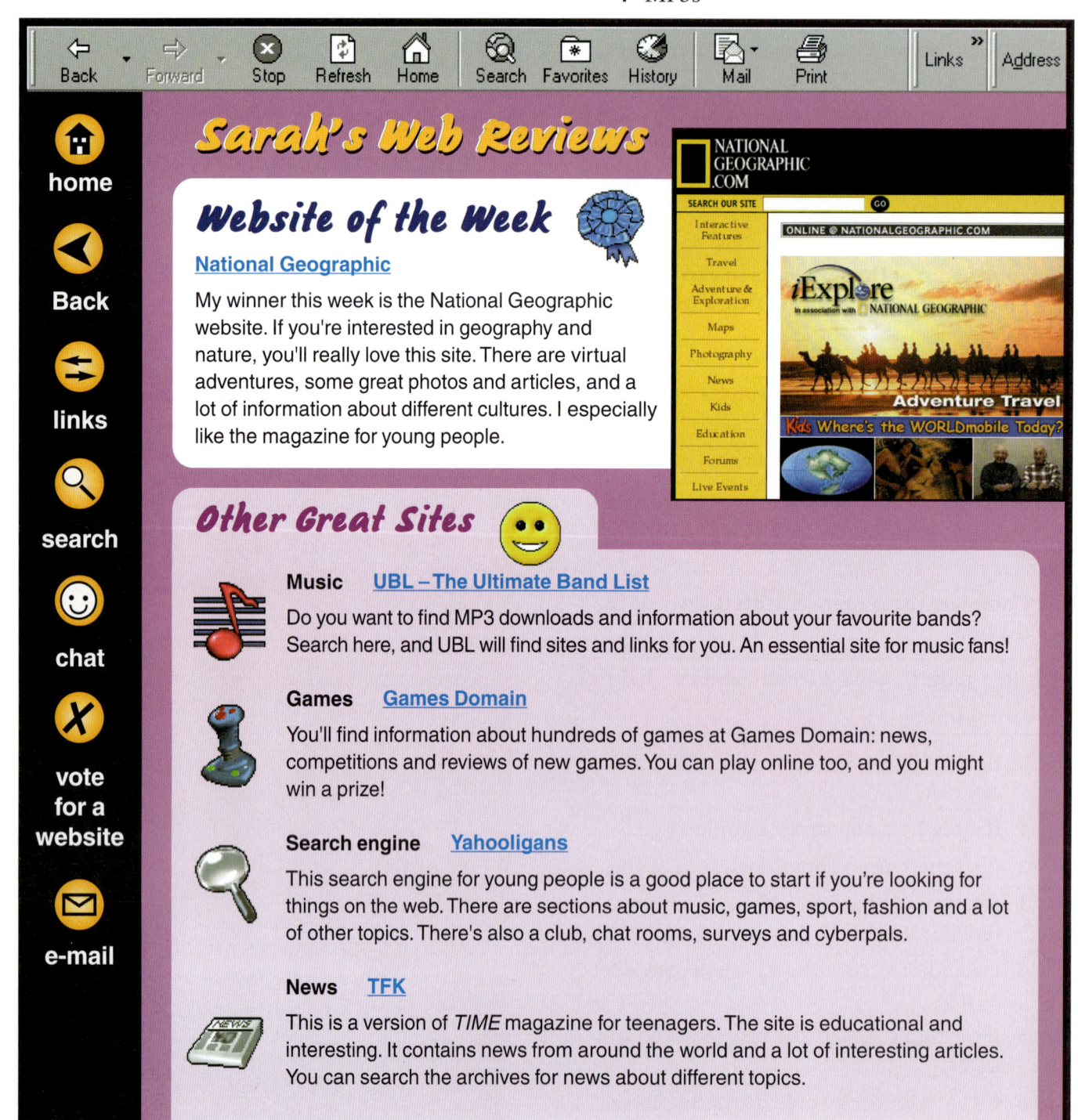

Sarah's Web Reviews

Website of the Week

National Geographic

My winner this week is the National Geographic website. If you're interested in geography and nature, you'll really love this site. There are virtual adventures, some great photos and articles, and a lot of information about different cultures. I especially like the magazine for young people.

Other Great Sites

Music   UBL – The Ultimate Band List

Do you want to find MP3 downloads and information about your favourite bands? Search here, and UBL will find sites and links for you. An essential site for music fans!

Games   Games Domain

You'll find information about hundreds of games at Games Domain: news, competitions and reviews of new games. You can play online too, and you might win a prize!

Search engine   Yahooligans

This search engine for young people is a good place to start if you're looking for things on the web. There are sections about music, games, sport, fashion and a lot of other topics. There's also a club, chat rooms, surveys and cyberpals.

News   TFK

This is a version of *TIME* magazine for teenagers. The site is educational and interesting. It contains news from around the world and a lot of interesting articles. You can search the archives for news about different topics.

Listening

3 Listen to some people talking about computers and the internet. Match names 1–3 with words a–c.

1 Kate   a chat room
2 Carol   b websites
3 Emma   c e-mail

4 Complete the sentences. Then listen again and check your answers.

1 The *National Geographic* website has a special section for …
2 Kate often prints …
3 Carol and her daughter send each other …
4 Carol's husband, Terry, doesn't like computers because he's worried about …
5 Emma can only use her computer for …
6 Emma's mother doesn't like chat rooms because Emma doesn't …

Writing

Organizing ideas: mind maps

5 Sarah is designing a website. Complete her mind map with words from the box.

> Fan   musicians   CDs   ~~Introduction~~   History

Home page
Introduction to electronic music. Map of the website.

Other pages
(1) …… of techno music. Interviews with (2) …… . News and reviews of CDs.

My website: Techno!

Images and downloads
Covers of my favourite (3) …… . Videos and photos of bands.

Links
Home pages of bands. (4) …… club pages.

6 Sarah wrote a description of her website. Order parts a–e.

a On some of these pages there are video and audio files, as well as photos of bands. You can download these if you want.

b On the home page there's an introduction and a map of the website. This will help you to find everything you need.

c Finally, you'll find links to different bands' websites, and there are also links to a few fan clubs. I'm sure you'll enjoy the site. Please visit soon!

d The name of my website is 'Techno!' and it's about electronic dance music. If you like techno or garage music, you should visit my site.

e On other pages you'll find a short history of electronic dance music and some interviews with musicians. There are also sections with news about my favourite bands and reviews of new CDs.

7 Plan a website. Think of a subject that you like and make a mind map of ideas for your site.

8 Write a description of your website. Use your mind map and some of the expressions in the box.

> If you like … , you should …
> On other pages you'll find …
> There are sections about …
> There are some great …
> You can download …   There are links to …

My website is called 'The Premiership' and it's about English football.

Finished?

Plan a website about your school.

Progress Check 7

Computers

1 Write the names of the objects.

1 mouse

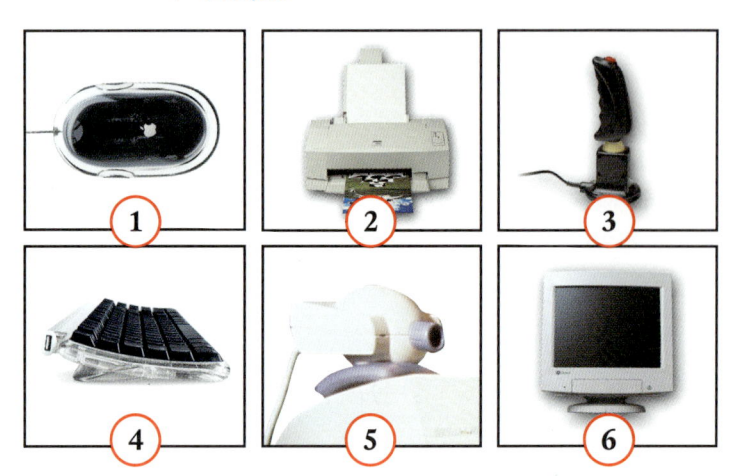

The internet

2 Match 1–6 with a–f to make words or phrases.

1 on	a room
2 e-	b site
3 web	c load
4 search	d mail
5 down	e line
6 chat	f engine

will and might

3 Look at the questionnaire and write Lucy's opinions about the future. Use *will*, *won't* and *might*.

People might live on the moon.

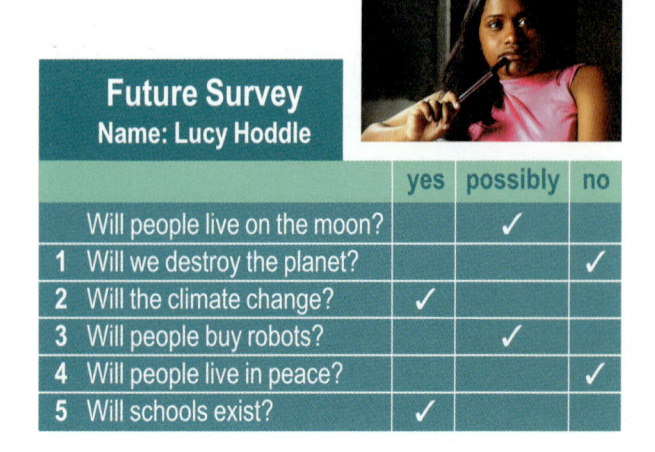

Future Survey
Name: Lucy Hoddle

	yes	possibly	no
Will people live on the moon?		✓	
1 Will we destroy the planet?			✓
2 Will the climate change?	✓		
3 Will people buy robots?		✓	
4 Will people live in peace?			✓
5 Will schools exist?	✓		

First conditional

4 Complete the sentences. Use the first conditional.

If Castle Master *touches* the red button, the door *won't open*.

1 If he …… (touch) the green button, the door …… (open).
2 If the door …… (not open), he …… (not escape).
3 If the door …… (open), he …… (find) a spaceship.
4 If he …… (steal) the spaceship, he …… (escape).
5 If he …… (escape), he …… (save) his planet.
6 If he …… (not succeed), his people …… (die).

Second conditional

5 Complete the sentences with the words in the box.

> I'd   didn't   ~~learn~~   buy   would   bought   liked

If we had computers in class, we'd *learn* more.

1 If I designed a website, it …… be excellent.
2 I'd visit the 'Techno!' website if I …… electronic dance music.
3 If I didn't play computer games, …… study more.
4 We'd be bored if we …… go to school.
5 I'd …… a new computer if I had some money.
6 If I …… a laptop computer, I wouldn't take it to school.

8 Rules

Have a look!

Find the pages where you:
- read about a girl's experience at school.
- listen to people talking about school rules.
- do a questionnaire.

Vocabulary

Legal and illegal

1. Look at the words in the box. Which of the things are in the pictures?

   > slavery   bullying   smoking   alcohol
   > gangs   drugs   graffiti   hunting   guns
   > protest

2. Guess the meaning of the other words in the box. Then listen and repeat.

   VOCABULARY PAGE 127, 8.1

3. Decide which things should be legal or illegal. Write the words in two columns.

Legal	Illegal
	slavery

Speaking

4. Work in pairs. Exchange opinions. Which things should be legal or illegal?

   A: *Do you think that slavery should be legal?*
   B: *No, I don't.*

8a Banned!

Reading

1 Listen and read. Then put a–e in chronological order.

a Women were allowed to vote in New Zealand.
b People weren't allowed to drink alcohol in the USA.
c King Edward III banned all sport in England.
d The British government banned slavery.
e The British government banned handguns.

2 Read the text again and answer the questions.

1 Were the prohibition laws popular?
2 Why did King Edward III ban all sports?
3 Are the gun laws stricter in the USA or in your country?
4 Where are slaves still bought and sold?
5 Who were the suffragettes?
6 Where is it illegal for women to drive?

Society's rules: then and now

Has society improved its rules? Read our report and make your own decision.

	Then	Now
alcohol 	The US government banned the consumption of alcohol in the early 1920s. The 'prohibition' laws were unpopular and people continued to drink. They made alcohol and they went to secret, illegal bars.	Laws about alcohol vary for different nationalities and cultures. For example, Muslims aren't allowed to drink alcohol. Perhaps that's a good idea. Police say that alcohol is a factor in 40% of traffic accidents.
weapons 	In the past, it was normal to carry a weapon, and children often fought in wars. King Edward III banned all sports in England in 1349 because he wanted men to spend more time training with weapons.	Children still fight in wars today, and personal weapons are still popular. The British government banned all handguns in 1997, but you can buy a handgun in the USA if you're 18. You don't need a licence.
slavery 	In the 19th century, you could buy slaves at markets. Britain, Spain and the USA were centres of the slave trade. Slavery was legal in Britain until 1835.	Slavery still exists in some countries. A slave in Mauritania costs $35. In Sudan people sometimes kidnap and sell children. Governments are trying to stop the slave trade.
women's rights 	At the end of the 19th century, women started to protest because they weren't allowed to vote. In Britain these women were called 'suffragettes'. More than 1,000 suffragettes went to prison because of their protests. In 1893, New Zealand became the first country where all women could vote.	There is still inequality around the world. In Saudi Arabia, for example, it is illegal for women to drive. In Iran, women are not allowed to go to football matches.

Exploring grammar

Permission: *can*, *could* and *be allowed to*

We use *can*, *could* and *be allowed to* to talk about permission.

3 Look at the text in exercise 1 again. Complete the table.

can / could
We use **can** and **could** + verb, without **to**.
Present: You **can buy** a gun in the USA.
Past: You **(1)** …… slaves at markets.
be allowed to
We use **be allowed to** + verb.
Present: Muslims **(2)** …… alcohol.
Past: They **weren't allowed to** vote.

GRAMMAR PAGE 122

4 Complete the text with the correct form of *be allowed to*. Then listen and check.

Sultan Murad IV was a cruel monarch. His people weren't allowed to drink coffee or alcohol. He banned tobacco in 1633. His soldiers **(1)** …… smoke, and he personally executed guilty men. The Sultan invented the laws, but he didn't obey them: he **(2)** …… smoke and drink!

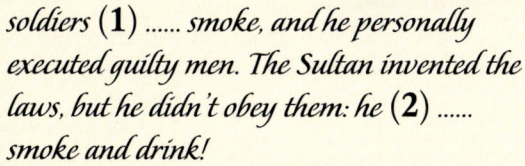

There are still some strange laws today. In Singapore, for example, you can eat chewing gum at home, but you **(3)** …… eat it on public transport.

In some American cities, teenagers **(4)** …… be on the streets until 10 p.m., but after that they **(5)** …… go out. And in Britain, you **(6)** …… have a TV, but only if you buy a TV licence!

5 Write true sentences with words from boxes a and b. Use *can*, *can't*, *could*, *couldn't* and *be allowed to*.

a
- When I was
- Now I'm
- When people are

b
five	ten
fourteen	fifteen
sixteen	seventeen
eighteen	twenty-one

When I was fourteen, I couldn't stay out after midnight.

Pronunciation

/ə/ and weak forms 2

6 Listen and repeat.

1 You can /kən/ buy a gun.
2 You could /kəd/ buy slaves.
3 Britain and Spain were /wə/ centres of the slave trade.
4 It was /wəz/ normal.
5 There are /ə/ still some strange laws.

7 Listen and repeat. Do you hear a or b?

	a		b	
1	can	/kən/	can't	/kɑːnt/
2	could	/kəd/	couldn't	/ˈkʊd(ə)nt/
3	are	/ə/	aren't	/ɑːnt/
4	was	/wəz/	wasn't	/ˈwəz(ə)nt/
5	were	/wə/	weren't	/wɜːnt/

Speaking

8 Work in pairs. Ask and answer questions about the ideas in exercise 5.

When you were fourteen, could you stay out after midnight?

Finished?

Invent your own strange laws.
You aren't allowed to wear red socks.

Unit 8 *Rules*

8b Strict or soft?

Reading

1 Do the questionnaire. Then look at the key.

Are you strict or soft?

Imagine that you are the parent of a teenage son and daughter of fourteen and fifteen years of age. Write a, b or c for each question. Then check the key at the bottom of the page.

1. Do your son and daughter have to help at home?
   - **a** Yes, thirty minutes every day.
   - **b** They have to do one or two jobs.
   - **c** No, they don't have to help. They're too young.

2. What is your attitude to their homework?
   - **a** I ask about their homework and I sometimes look at it.
   - **b** I ask about their homework, but I don't look at it.
   - **c** I don't ask about their homework. That's the teacher's job.

3. You haven't met your daughter's boyfriend. She's known him for two months.
   - **a** I have to meet him. I insist!
   - **b** I'm interested, but she doesn't have to bring him home.
   - **c** It's none of my business.

4. Your son wants to have a tattoo.
   - **a** No way.
   - **b** I ask him to wait for a month. Then he can ask me again.
   - **c** I don't mind, but he must pay for it.

5. Your daughter wants a TV in her bedroom.
   - **a** She can't have a TV in her room. It's anti-social.
   - **b** That's OK if she does her homework. But she mustn't watch TV all the time.
   - **c** Her room is a private place and she can do what she wants in it.

6. You've had an argument with your son. He was wrong, but he didn't apologize.
   - **a** I tell him that he isn't allowed to go out for a week.
   - **b** I talk to him later and ask him to apologize.
   - **c** He's too old for discipline now. He will never learn respect if he hasn't already learnt it.

7. You think that your son is missing classes at school.
   - **a** You follow him secretly and find out what he's doing.
   - **b** You check that everything is OK with your son and his tutor.
   - **c** He's old enough to make his own decisions.

Key

Mostly a answers:
Wow, you think that strict is best! But remember that it is a good idea to give people a little space and time to be individuals.

Mostly b answers:
Well done! You are firm but fair. You understand that young people need some control, but not too much. Parents have to be interested in their children, but they mustn't be too strict. You know that your parents haven't got an easy job!

Mostly c answers:
Oh, dear! You've got a strange attitude. Some people have to be responsible for others. Imagine if there was no control in the world!

Exploring grammar
Obligation: *have to* and *must*

We use *have to* and *must* when we talk about obligation.

2 Copy and complete the table. Find the negative forms in the text on page 82.

Affirmative		Negative
I / you / we / they	**have to**	(1) ......
he / she / it	**has to**	(2) ......

3 Read the rules about *have to* and *must*. Then look at the sentences about Kim and Mark. Choose the correct forms of the verbs.

Rules

1 **Must** and **mustn't** express an obligation.
   She **must** pay for it.
   She **mustn't** watch TV.

2 We use negative forms of **have to** when there is no obligation.
   You **don't have to** go. (No obligation)
   You **mustn't** go. (Obligation)

GRAMMAR PAGE 122

Kim's parents are very strict.
She **has to** / doesn't have to go shopping with them.
1 She **has to** / **doesn't have to** be home early.
2 She **mustn't** / **doesn't have to** play loud music.
3 She **mustn't** / **doesn't have to** wear trousers.

Mark's parents aren't strict.
4 He **mustn't** / **doesn't have to** help at home.
5 He **mustn't** / **doesn't have to** be home early.
6 He **has to** / **doesn't have to** clean his room.

Vocabulary
Household tasks and objects

4 Match the objects with the tasks in the box.

> wash the dishes   iron your clothes
> make coffee   cook   clean the floor
> wash your clothes

1 cooker
2 mop
3 washing machine
4 iron
5 dishwasher
6 coffee machine

5 Write true sentences with affirmative and negative forms of *have to*.

I don't have to wash my clothes.

1 My mother / iron my clothes.
2 I / wash the dishes every day.
3 My father / cook dinner.
4 I / clean the floor in the kitchen.
5 I / make coffee for my parents.

Speaking

6 Work in pairs. Ask and answer questions with the expressions in exercise 4.

A: *Do you have to cook dinner?*
B: *No, I don't.*

Finished?

Write more sentences about obligations.
My mum has to get up at six o'clock.

Unit 8 *Rules*

8c Rules

Reading

1 Look at the title of the article and the photos. Then guess which of the words in the box are in the article.

> rules bully fair weapon female
> protest uniform legal

2 Read the article and check your answers.

'Delighted' schoolgirl wins battle to wear trousers

A girl has won her battle to wear trousers at school. Jo Hale is fourteen years old and is a pupil at Whickham Secondary School in the north-east of England.

Jo wore trousers to primary school, but she wasn't allowed to wear them when she went to Whickham. Jo was unhappy because she was cold in a skirt in the winter, but the school didn't change its rules about uniforms. Jo said, 'If you are in class doing your work, what difference does it make if you are wearing trousers?'

Jo's mother, Claire, is a professor at the University of Leeds. She contacted the school because, in her opinion, the rules weren't fair. 'The female teachers can wear trousers but the students can't,' she said. 'Trousers are a more practical form of dress. They are warmer in winter and cheaper to wear than a skirt.'

Jo's mother and the school prepared to fight a legal battle, but then the school decided that the legal costs were too expensive, and they changed the rules.

Now Jo and the other girls at Whickham are allowed to wear trousers. Jo says that she's 'delighted'.

3 Read the article again. Are the sentences true or false? Explain your answers.

> There is still a battle about uniforms at Jo's school.
> *False. Jo won the battle.*

1 School rules are the same in primary and secondary schools.
2 Jo Hale prefers trousers because skirts are old-fashioned.
3 The school agreed with Jo's ideas.
4 Jo's mother didn't agree with the school rules.
5 The school wanted to change the rules.
6 The rules at Whickham have changed.

Speaking

4 Work in pairs. Discuss the list of rules. Do you agree with them or not?

A: Do you agree with number 1?
B: No, I don't.
A: Why not?

1 Students must wear a uniform.
2 Teachers have to respect students.
3 Students aren't allowed to chew gum.
4 Teachers mustn't shout.
5 Students aren't allowed to dye their hair.
6 Students have to carry special ID cards.

5 Think of your classes this year. Suggest more rules for next year's classes.

I think that students should always listen when the teacher is speaking.

Listening

6 Listen to the people in the photos. Where do they go to school?

Reuben   Aki   Wayne

7 Listen again and answer the questions.

1 Are bullies a big problem at Reuben's school?
2 How do students in Reuben's school decide their extra class rules?
3 Why do the students in Aki's school have to use certain roads?
4 What percentage of students in Washington have taken a gun to school?
5 Why does Wayne think that school uniforms are a good idea?

Writing

Expressing contrast: *however*, *although*, *but* and *on the other hand*

8 Translate the sentences.

1 We haven't got many problems here, **although** there are one or two bullies.
2 Some of my friends, **however**, prefer long hair or coloured hair.
3 Some people wore expensive clothes to school before, **but** now we all wear the same uniform.
4 I don't like the design. **On the other hand**, you don't have to think about what to wear.

9 Look at Reuben's ideas for new school rules. Match 1–4 with a–d.

1 Students are allowed to talk in class,
2 Students can decorate the classrooms,
3 Students over 15 can wear normal clothes.
4 Students don't have to do exams.

a although they have to pay for the paint.
b Their work, however, is assessed every week.
c but they mustn't interrupt another person.
d Younger students, on the other hand, must wear a uniform.

10 Think of ideas for school rules. Write about four of the topics in the box. Use *however*, *although*, *but* and *on the other hand*.

homework   choice of subjects   timetable
exams   mobile phones   uniforms

My ideas for school rules
We have to do homework, but the maximum ...

Finished?

Describe the perfect student.
The perfect student studies a lot.

Progress Check 8

Legal and illegal

1 Complete the sentences with the words in the box.

> drugs   alcohol   Hunting   graffiti
> Smoking   gun   ~~Slavery~~

Slavery was banned in England in 1835.

1 ...... cigarettes is bad for your health.
2 Some people say that ...... is artistic.
3 Cocaine and heroin are ....
4 Wine contains ....
5 A ...... is a type of weapon.
6 ...... some animals is illegal.

Household tasks and objects

2 Write the names of the objects in photos 1–6. Write the verbs for the objects.

1 dishwasher – wash the dishes

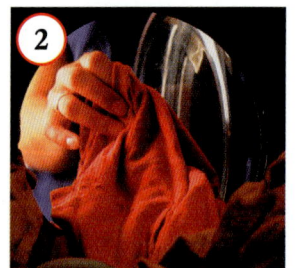

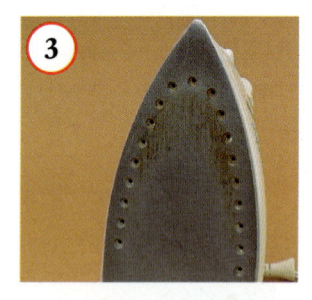

Permission: *can*, *could* and *be allowed to*

3 Choose the correct words.

> When I was at school, the rules were very strict. We **weren't allowed to** / **could** speak to other students in the class.
> We **(1) were allowed to** / **couldn't** speak to the teacher, but only if he or she asked a question. The teacher **(2) could** / **can't** use physical punishment and we **(3) couldn't** / **are allowed to** complain.
> Now things are very different. Young people **(4) can't** / **are allowed to** do what they like. When I was a child I **(5) wasn't allowed to** / **can't** do half the things that young people **(6) can't** / **can** do today.

have to and *must*

4 Complete the sentences with *have to*, *has to*, *doesn't have to* and *mustn't*.

Tessa has to wear a hat.

Tessa – police officer   David – pilot

Rules of the jobs

1 Tessa and David ...... wear a uniform.
2 David ...... drink alcohol when he's working.
3 David ...... cook meals on the plane.
4 Tessa ...... carry a weapon.
5 Tessa ...... forget her walkie-talkie.
6 Tessa and David ...... do difficult jobs.

The World of English 4

North Street (pages 88 and 89)

Revision: first conditional, second conditional, *have to, must*

Function: Giving opinions

1. What question does Maxine ask Rick?

Culture File (pages 90 and 91)

Topic: Youth culture: crazes

2. What's the name of this toy?

The Story of Pop (page 92)

Artist: Jimmy Cliff
Type of music: Ska and reggae
Song: I can see clearly now

3. What is Jimmy Cliff's real name?

North Street

A difficult question

1

Josie Look, Maxine, there's Chris Hall. Wow! He's really gorgeous. And he's got a motorbike.
Maxine Mmm. Maybe if he had less money, he'd be friendlier. He's not my type.
Josie Who's your type then? You fancy Rick, don't you?
Maxine Josie, if you tell him, I'll be furious. But yes, he's got a nice personality and that's important.

2

Josie I think that money's really important. Don't you agree?
Maxine No, I don't agree with you.
Josie That's interesting. Why's that?
Maxine Well, because money can't buy you love.
Josie Maybe you're right. Let's ask Rick. Hey, Rick. Come here!

3

Rick Hi, Josie. Hi, Max. What can I do for you?
Josie We were talking about love and money.
Rick Don't mention money. I'm completely broke.
Maxine No, Rick, the question is: What's the most important thing in life?
Rick Difficult question. I'm not sure. I'll have to think about it.

4 *Later that day ...*

Maxine Hey, Rick. What's your answer, then?
Rick What? Oh, yeah – the most important thing is ... a skateboard. If you've got a good skateboard, you'll always be happy!
Maxine Thanks, Rick. I must remember that.
Rick You're welcome. Any time!

Reading

1 Read and listen to North Street. Then answer the questions.

1 Does Josie like Chris?
2 Why does Maxine prefer Rick?
3 What does Maxine think about love and money?
4 Has Rick got much money?
5 What's the most important thing in Rick's life?

Useful expressions

2 Find the expressions in the story. Then check their meaning.

1 He's not my type.
2 You fancy Rick, don't you?
3 Maybe you're right.
4 I'm completely broke.

Dialogue

Giving opinions

3 Look at this extract from North Street. Listen and repeat. Concentrate on your rhythm and intonation.

A: I think that money's really important. Don't you agree?
B: No, I don't agree with you.
A: That's interesting. Why's that?
B: Well, because money can't buy you love.
A: Maybe you're right. Let's ask Rick.

4 Read the opinions. Then write *Yes*, *No*, or *I'm not sure* for each opinion.

Women work more than men. *Yes.*
1 Football is really boring.
2 It's important to learn a foreign language.
3 Classical music is terrible.
4 There's life on other planets.

5 In pairs, discuss the opinions in exercise 4. Use exercise 3 as a model. Substitute the blue words and use the expressions in the box.

Yes, I agree.   No, I disagree.
I'm not really sure.

A: I think that women work more than men. Don't you agree?
B: Yes, I agree.
A: That's interesting. Why's that?
B: Well, because my mother has got a full-time job, and she does most of the housework, too.
A: Maybe you're right. Let's ask Jack.

The World of English 4

Culture File 4

Youth culture: crazes

1 Look at the pictures and answer the questions.
1. Which of these things are popular in your country?
2. Were any of them popular in the past?
3. Have you ever tried any of these activities?

inline skates   pogo stick   skateboard   yoyo   frisbee   hula hoop

2 Read the text. Which objects in exercise 1 does it mention?

The latest craze: Made in the USA

When something becomes fashionable very quickly, we say that it's a 'craze'. The latest craze is sometimes a style of clothes or a hairstyle. Sometimes it is a game or a TV programme. In the 20th century a lot of crazes started in the USA and then became popular in other parts of the world. American youth culture has spread through tourism, TV, films, magazines and music videos.

One of the biggest crazes was the hula hoop. They're not as popular now, but in the 1950s hula hoops were a sensation. An American company called Wham-O started to make plastic hoops as toys, and in the USA they sold 100 million hoops in a year – crazes are fun, and they are also big business.

Frisbees were another Wham-O product. Some say that the idea for frisbees started in the factory of the Frisbee Baking Company in Connecticut, USA. Workers there threw metal pans to each other during their breaks. Two businessmen made a plastic version of the flying pans, and sold their product to Wham-O. They became a big success.

So businesses usually help to create a craze. Yoyos are another example. In the Philippines, where its name means 'comeback', the yoyo was a popular toy in the 1920s, but it didn't become a global craze until an American called Donald Duncan bought the idea and sold it to the world. 100 million people bought yoyos in 1962 and 1963.

Most crazes come and go, but sometimes they survive. When the big skateboard boom started in California in 1965, many parents and authorities said that the boards were dangerous, and they banned them in some areas. But the boards became popular again and they are still an important part of youth culture today.

3 Read the text again and answer the questions.
1. How did crazes from the USA spread to other countries?
2. Which company sold hula hoops and frisbees?
3. Where did people throw pans as a game?
4. Were yoyos originally from the USA?
5. Why did people want to ban skateboards?

4 Listen to two British teenagers, Simon and Anna, talking about crazes. What do they talk about most – a, b, c or d?

a. computer games
b. skateboards
c. Clothes and designer labels
d. TV programmes

5 Listen again and answer the questions.
1. Which teenager likes American TV programmes?
2. Does Simon like streetstyle skating or freestyle skating?
3. Why does Simon always take his skateboard with him?
4. Does Simon skateboard in competitions?
5. What style of clothes does Anna like?
6. What's the problem with this type of clothing?

Project

Make a poster about a craze or fashion in your country at the moment. Choose a subject from the box or use your own ideas.

> TV programmes   toys and games
> clothing and footwear   pop groups
> TV / film characters   computer games

Include information about:
- where and when it started.
- why it is popular.
- if it will be popular for a long time.

Include photos and drawings.

The Story of Pop 4

Ska and reggae

1 Read and listen. Then answer the questions.

1. How did ska music originate?
2. Which is faster, reggae or ska music?
3. Which instruments are important in reggae?
4. How old was Jimmy Cliff when he had his first hit?
5. Why was Jimmy Cliff important for reggae music?

2 Complete the song with the words in the box. Then listen and check your answers.

> nothing   rainbow   skies   pain
> obstacles   ~~rain~~   feelings   clouds

(Verse 1)
I can see clearly now the *rain* is gone
I can see all (**1**) ...... in my way
Gone are the dark (**2**) ...... that had me blind
It's gonna be a bright (bright), bright (bright), sunshiny day (x 2).

(Verse 2)
I think I can make it now the (**3**) ...... is gone
All of the bad (**4**) ...... have disappeared
Here is the (**5**) ...... I've been hoping for
It's gonna be a bright (bright), bright (bright), sunshiny day.

Look all around, there's (**6**) ...... but blue skies
Look straight ahead, there's nothing but blue (**7**) ......

(Repeat verse 1)
It's gonna be a bright (bright), bright (bright), sunshiny day (x 4).

Glossary
gonna = going to
make it = succeed or survive

Ska and reggae

Music from the USA was popular in many parts of the world in the 1950s and '60s.

Jamaican musicians combined rhythm and blues with their own musical ideas, and the result was a fast dance music called 'ska'. Later, they invented 'reggae'. Reggae is a slower version of ska – some people say that ska was too fast for the hot Caribbean climate of Jamaica! The bass is a strong element of reggae, and the guitar and drum sounds are unique.

reggae musicians

Jimmy Cliff

Jimmy Cliff (real name James Chambers) was born in Jamaica in 1948. At the age of 14 he went to see a record producer and sang for him. The producer was impressed and paid for him to record two songs. One of the songs became a hit in Jamaica and this started Jimmy's career.
He travelled to Europe, Africa and South America, becoming one of the first international reggae stars. *I can see clearly now* was a hit for Jimmy in 1993.

9 Money

Have a look!

Find the pages where you:
- listen to information about making money.
- write about your life as a millionaire.
- do a coin quiz.

Vocabulary

Money

1 Match the words in the box with pictures 1–10. Then listen and check.

> bank   banknote   cash machine
> coin   credit card   foreign currency
> purse   gold   safe   wallet

1 foreign currency

VOCABULARY PAGE 128, 9.1

Speaking

2 Work in groups. Ask and answer the questions.

1. How many cents are there in a euro?
2. What are the currencies of the UK and the USA?
3. How many other foreign currencies can you name?
4. What did people use as money before banknotes and coins?
5. Are people happier when they've got a lot of money?

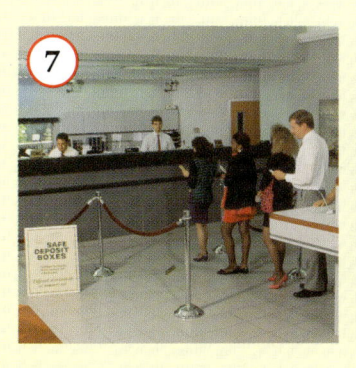

93

9a Making money

Listening

1 Put the pictures in order. Then listen and check.

1b

The production of banknotes

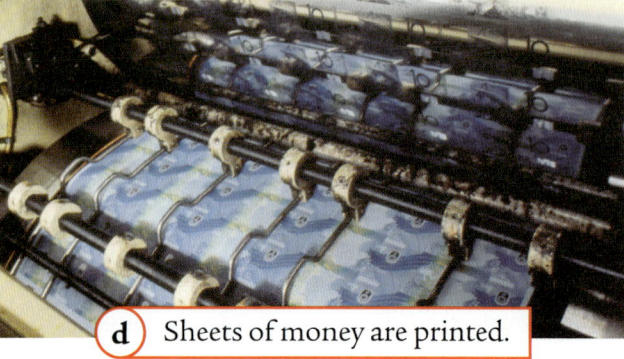

a — The sheets are checked.

b — The notes are designed.

c — The sheets are cut.

d — Sheets of money are printed.

2 Listen again and answer the questions.
1. Who designs the banknotes?
2. How many sheets of money are printed every hour?
3. How are the notes counted?
4. Where is the money stored before it is sent to the banks?
5. Are old banknotes kept?

The old banknotes are destroyed.

Exploring grammar

The passive: present simple

We use the passive to talk about processes.

We form the present simple passive with the present simple of *be* + past participle.

The object in an active sentence becomes the subject in a passive sentence.

People make **money** here. (Active)
Money is made here. (Passive)

3 Complete the table with *is*, *isn't* and *are*.

Affirmative
Banknotes **are designed** (by artists).
The design (1) ...... **transferred** to metal plates.

Negative
Money (2) ...... **counted** by people.
They **aren't** all **designed** by the same person.

Questions
Where (3) ...... the money **stored**?
How (4) ...... the notes **counted**?

GRAMMAR ▶ PAGE 122

9a

4 Complete the text with the present simple passive form of the verbs in brackets.

- special paper
- serial number
- hologram
- security strip

Forgery!

Sometimes banknotes *are copied* or printed by criminals. These illegal notes are called 'forgeries'. It's difficult to make good forgeries, because special paper and serial numbers (**1**) ...... (use) when real notes (**2**) ...... (print). Also, when a banknote (**3**) ...... (design), the artist draws a very detailed picture with fine lines. Usually copies (**4**) ...... (discover) by the public or the police because they (**5**) ...... (not make) very well. Holograms and security strips (**6**) ...... (not include) on most forgeries.

Vocabulary

Production and consumption

5 Find the meaning of the verbs. Then write the past simple and past participle forms.

design – designed – designed
make – made – made

1 buy	4 consume	7 recycle
2 grow	5 build	8 mine
3 sell	6 produce	9 print

VOCABULARY PAGE 128, 9.2

IRREGULAR VERBS INSIDE BACK COVER

6 Complete the sentences with the correct form of the present simple passive. Then choose answers.

Consumer facts

1. How many burgers *are consumed* (consume) every day in the USA?
   - a 1.5 million
   - b 15 million
2. How many CDs ...... (sell) in the USA every day?
   - a 2 million
   - b 20 million
3. Where ...... most trainers ...... (make)?
   - a Asia
   - b Europe
4. How much rubbish ...... (produce) in the world every day?
   - a 2 million tonnes
   - b 2,000 tonnes
5. How many cars ...... (buy) in the world every minute?
   - a 7
   - b 70
6. How much gold ...... (mine) in the world every day?
   - a 63 kilos
   - b 6,300 kilos

Pronunciation

/j/

7 Listen and repeat.

1 you	3 USA	5 usually
2 use	4 euro	6 produce

8 Listen and repeat.

Do you usually use euros in the USA or Europe?

Finished?

Write sentences about the things that are made in your region.

Ships are built in ...
Coal is mined in ...

9b The story of money

Reading

1 Do the quiz.

Coin Quiz

1 John F Kennedy was assassinated in 1963. He was the president of …
   a Scotland.
   b the USA.

2 This Argentinian coin was made of gold in 1888. What are modern coins made of?
   a cheap metals
   b bronze

3 A new European currency was introduced in 2001. What is the name of the currency?
   a euro
   b europa

4 In 2002 the World Cup was held in Japan and South Korea. Who were the winners of the competition?
   a Brazil
   b France

5 This Egyptian coin shows the pyramids at Giza. When were the pyramids built?
   a 450 years ago
   b 4,500 years ago

6 Coloured coins weren't produced until recently. Where was this coin made?
   a Canada
   b Japan

7 The design on this coin was made by artist Leonardo Da Vinci. Where was he born?
   a The USA
   b Italy

8 Early money wasn't always made in regular shapes. Where was this 'knife coin' discovered?
   a China
   b Australia

Exploring grammar
The passive: past simple

We form the past simple passive with the past simple of *be* + past participle.

2 Complete the table with more sentences from the quiz in exercise 1.

Affirmative
John F Kennedy **was assassinated**.
(1) ......
Negative
Early money **wasn't made** in regular shapes.
(2) ......
Questions
When **were** the pyramids **built**?
(3) ......

GRAMMAR ▶ PAGE 122

3 Complete the text with the correct form of the past simple passive.

The story of money – frequently asked questions

What system *was used* (use) before money?
Products and services (1) ...... (exchange) in a system called 'barter'.

What things (2) ...... (use) as money before notes and coins?
Precious materials (3) ...... (use), like shells or salt. Coins (4) ...... (not produce) until much later.

Where (5) ...... the first coins ...... (discover)?
The first coins (6) ...... (find) in Turkey. They (7) ...... (make) more than 2,500 years ago.

When (8) ...... banknotes ...... (invent)?
They (9) ...... (not invent) until 1,000 years ago. The first banknotes (10) ...... (make) in China.

4 Convert the sentences on the poster from active to passive. Then listen and check.

1 Only one new hospital was built.

WANTED FOR CORRUPTION!
President I.M.A. Grabber

Last year, the government spent **$** billions of **your** money!

1. They built only one new hospital.
2. They built three palaces for the president.
3. They closed ten schools.
4. They created no new jobs.
5. They spent a lot of money in expensive restaurants.

5 Imagine that you were the president last year. Write about how you spent your country's money. Use the past simple passive of the verbs in the box.

> build   close   create   produce   spend

Billions of euros were spent on teenagers.

Speaking

6 Work in groups. Read out your sentences and vote for the best president.

Finished?
Think of true and false sentences for a quiz. Use the past simple passive form of the verbs in the box.

> build   make   record   rule
> win   write

The last European football championship was won by Ireland. (False.)

Unit 9 *Money*

9c Teenage millionaires

Reading

1 Read and listen. Which of these people has not had problems with money?
   a Jennifer Capriati
   b Macaulay Culkin
   c Daniel Radcliffe

2 Read the text again and answer the questions.
   1 When did Jennifer Capriati become rebellious?
   2 Did Jennifer play tennis again after her parents separated?
   3 Who controls Macaulay Culkin's money now?
   4 What do people need if they are young and rich?
   5 What does Daniel Radcliffe think about fame?

THE PRICE OF FAME

Jennifer Capriati, a teenage champion.

Jennifer Capriati, a champion again at twenty-four.

Many of us dream of making millions, but some young stars quickly learn that money can't always buy you love or happiness …

After becoming a tennis professional when she was only fourteen years old, Jennifer Capriati soon became a millionaire. Her parents, however, argued constantly about her money and eventually they separated. Jennifer became very rebellious. She had problems with the police and was arrested twice. She didn't become a champion again until she was twenty-four.

There are also victims in the world of cinema. Macaulay Culkin became a successful film star at the age of ten, and was paid millions of dollars. But his parents argued. Macaulay suffered from depression and he had problems at school. He has now got a business manager who looks after his money.

So teenage millionaires need a strong family and a good attitude. When Daniel Radcliffe was chosen for the part of Harry Potter, he suddenly became the most famous actor on the planet. He also became rich. He has said, 'I think a bit of fame will probably just be fun, and I won't mind it. But I still want to lead a normal life with my friends.' And his parents? 'My mum and dad have just told me to enjoy it,' says Daniel. Well, good luck to him!

Macaulay Culkin, the actor, aged ten.

Daniel Radcliffe as Harry Potter.

Speaking

3 Imagine that you are a teenage millionaire. In pairs, ask and answer the questions for the footballer or the film star.

> A: *When you were still at school, you were offered a contract by a famous football team. How old were you?*
>
> B: *I was fourteen.*

Questions for a footballer

When you were still at school, you were offered a contract by a famous football team.

1. How old were you?
2. Which team was it?

Then you were chosen to play for the national team.

3. How many goals did you score in your first international match?

Now you're paid a fortune every month and you're very happy.

4. How much do you earn?
5. Who is your new boyfriend/girlfriend?

Questions for a film star

When you were still at school, you were discovered by a famous film director.

1. How old were you?
2. Who did you act with in your first film?

Then you were nominated for three Oscars in three years.

3. How many Oscars did you win?

Now you're paid a fortune for each film you make and you're very happy.

4. How much are you paid for each film?
5. Who is your new boyfriend/girlfriend?

Study skills
Improving your communication skills

When we ask questions, we usually react to people's answers.

4 Listen to an interview with a young film star and look at the expressions in the box. Which do you hear?

> Really?   That's interesting.   Oh yes?
> Oh no!   That's a pity.   Oh, go on!
> Fantastic!   Congratulations!

5 Repeat your interviews from exercise 3. Try to use some expressions from exercise 4.

Writing
An autobiography: organizing a paragraph

We use the time references *when*, *then* and *now* to help us to put ideas in the correct order.

6 Put the sentences in order.

a **Then** Macaulay's life changed. His parents argued about his money.

b **When** Macaulay Culkin was ten years old, he became a film star.

c **Now** he's got a business manager who looks after his money.

7 Complete the text with *now*, *when* and *then*.

(**1**) ...... I was fifteen, I was offered a contract by Arsenal football club. (**2**) ...... I was chosen to play for the England team. I scored a goal in my first international! (**3**) ...... I'm paid £100,000 every week and I'm married to Britney Spears.

8 Write about your life as a millionaire actor or footballer. Use *when*, *then* and *now*.

> *When I was twelve, I was discovered by a famous film director. Then ...*

Finished?

Write another paragraph about the problems you had as a teenage millionaire.

My problems started when I was ...

Unit 9 *Money*

Progress Check 9

Money

1 Write the words.

You can take money from this machine.
c *ash* m *achine*

1 Money made from metal. c ......
2 'Plastic' money. c ...... c ......
3 An expensive metal. g ......
4 Money made from paper. b ......
5 Money from other countries. f ...... c ......

Production and consumption

2 Complete the table with the infinitive, past simple and past participle forms of the verbs.

Infinitive	Past simple	Past participle
build	*built*	built
buy	bought	(1) ......
(2)	consumed	consumed
design	(3)	designed
grow	grew	(4) ......
(5)	made	made
produce	(6)	produced
recycle	recycled	(7) ......
(8)	sold	sold

The passive: present simple

3 Complete the questions with the words in the box. Then answer the questions.

is ~~are~~ made are Were was

Where *are* coins made?
Coins are made in a mint.

1 What currency ...... used in your country?
2 Where ...... euros used?
3 ...... banknotes first made in Turkey?
4 What are credit cards ...... of?
5 What system ...... used before money?

The passive: past simple

4 Complete the text. Use the past simple passive form of the verbs.

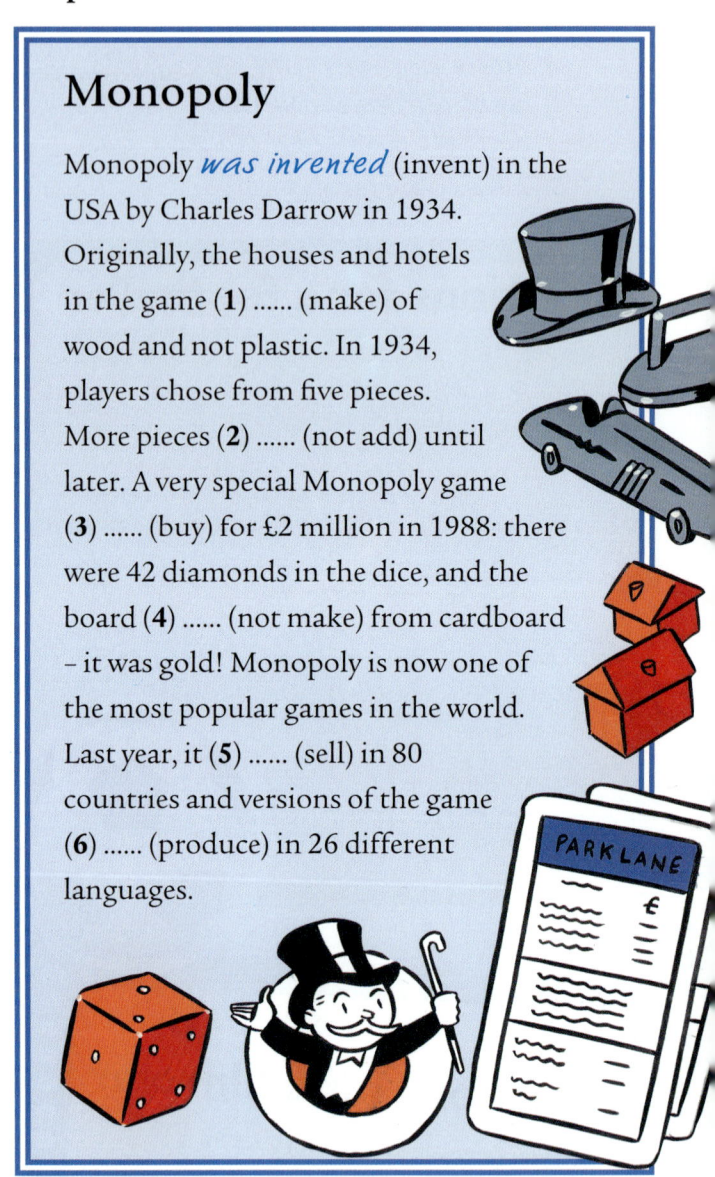

Monopoly

Monopoly *was invented* (invent) in the USA by Charles Darrow in 1934. Originally, the houses and hotels in the game (1) ...... (make) of wood and not plastic. In 1934, players chose from five pieces. More pieces (2) ...... (not add) until later. A very special Monopoly game (3) ...... (buy) for £2 million in 1988: there were 42 diamonds in the dice, and the board (4) ...... (not make) from cardboard – it was gold! Monopoly is now one of the most popular games in the world. Last year, it (5) ...... (sell) in 80 countries and versions of the game (6) ...... (produce) in 26 different languages.

5 Read the text in exercise 4. Write questions for these answers.

Where was Monopoly invented?
Monopoly was invented in the USA.

1 By Charles Darrow.
2 In 1934.
3 No, they weren't. They were made of wood.
4 It was bought in 1988.
5 Yes, it was produced in 26 different languages.

10 News and views

Have a look!
Find the pages where you:
- write a story about a dramatic photo.
- listen to an interview about news stories.
- read a strange story from the press.

Vocabulary
News topics

1 Match the words in the box with pictures 1–8. Then listen and check.

> economics and business   ecology
> politics   health and medicine   lifestyle
> war and disasters   science and technology
> culture and entertainment

2 Which topics interest you most? Make a list.

1 culture and entertainment

VOCABULARY PAGE 128, 10.1

101

10a True stories

Reading

1 Read the true stories. Then match 1–4 with pictures a–d.

Listening

2 Guess the ending for each story. Choose a or b. Then listen and check.

True stories

1 A sticky story

Police in Florida yesterday rescued a man called Gemini Wink, 26, of Louisville, Kentucky. He had gone to photograph wildlife in a National Park, but he got lost and decided to sleep in a tree. When police found Mr Wink, he was attached to the tree with adhesive tape.

He had used the tape:
a as protection against ants.
b so that he wouldn't fall and be eaten by crocodiles.

2 The big kiss

Dror Orpaz and Karmit Tsubera were receiving medical attention yesterday in Tel Aviv, Israel. They had won a marathon kissing competition in the main square of the city, but they had to go to hospital because they were both suffering from exhaustion. The competition was organized by a toothpaste company. Three hundred couples had started kissing on Monday at 8.30 p.m. and by 3 p.m. on Tuesday there were only two couples left. Twelve hours later Dror and Karmit won first prize: a trip around the world and US $2,500 cash.

They had kissed for:
a 30 hours and 30 minutes.
b 40 hours and 45 minutes.

3 Marry me (please, please, please …)

Beverley Redman is planning a honeymoon in Hawaii now that she has finally agreed to marry her partner, Keith. They have been together for twenty-four years, but Beverley had never accepted Keith's proposals of marriage. She had always given excuses because she was scared that the relationship would end in divorce.

Before Beverley accepted, Keith had proposed:
a more than 8,000 times.
b on his knees with a platinum ring.

4 Sad man misses big prize

Last weekend, Robert Kronk was a little sad. Thirteen of his colleagues at work in Ohio had won a lottery prize of US $295.7 million!

Each person in the group received a lot of money, but Robert didn't celebrate with them. He had always played the lottery with his colleagues, but he left the group three months before they won the big prize.

He left the group because:
a he had won a prize on another lottery.
b the group had selected their numbers with a computer, but Mr Kronk wanted to choose the numbers personally.

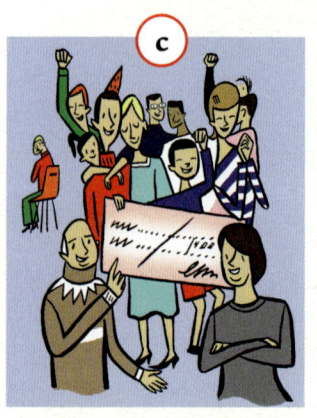

Exploring grammar
Past perfect

We use the past perfect to talk about an action in the past, which happened before another action in the past.

3 Read the rule and examples. Then find three more examples of the past perfect in the stories on page 102.

> We form the past perfect with **had** or **hadn't** + past participle.
>
> (1) He **had gone** to a National Park, but he got lost.
>
> (2) He left the group because he **had won** a prize on another lottery.

GRAMMAR PAGE 123

IRREGULAR VERBS INSIDE BACK COVER

4 Complete the story. Use the past perfect.

■ The longest run ■

In 1966, Shiro Kanakuri completed an Olympic marathon in a record time, 54 years, 8 months, 6 days, 8 hours, 32 minutes and 20.3 seconds after he *had started* the marathon!

He started the marathon in the 1912 Olympics in Stockholm. Unfortunately, he started to feel tired after he (1) …… (run) the first few kilometres of the race. Kanakuri stopped running because he (2) …… (see) some people having a party in their garden. He decided to have a drink with them. Sadly, he had to return home to Japan because he was too ill to complete the marathon because he (3) …… (drink) too much.

In 1966, he returned to the same place where he (4) …… (stop) running the race in 1912. This time, he ran until he completed the marathon. His wife, six children and ten grandchildren who (5) …… (wait) a long time for him to finish, were all very proud. At last, Kanakuri finished the race that he (6) …… (begin) more than 54 years earlier.

5 Invent explanations for these situations. Complete the sentences. Use the past perfect.

The musician was unhappy because *his guitar had exploded*.

1 My friends were celebrating because …… .
2 The men were in the newspaper because …… .
3 The girl was angry because …… .
4 The teacher was smiling because …… .
5 The film star was in prison because …… .
6 The athlete was happy because …… .

Pronunciation
-ed

6 Listen and repeat.

/d/	/t/	/ɪd/
rescued	attached	wanted

7 Complete the table from exercise 6 with the words in the box. Listen and check.

> accepted   called   worked   arrived
> started   kissed   stopped   completed

GRAMMAR PAGE 123

Speaking

8 Work in pairs. Ask and answer questions about the people in exercise 5.

> A: Why was the musician unhappy?
>
> B: The musician was unhappy because his guitar had exploded.

Finished?

Write a story about one of the situations in exercise 5.

The musician was unhappy because his guitar had exploded. He was playing in a big concert when …

10b Exclusive!

Reading

1 Read and listen. Then choose the best title, a, b or c.

a Sue and Bruno. Looking for another house!
b Footballer Bruno wants to go to Hollywood.
c Sue and Bruno. Happy in the mansion, but no plans for a family.

2 Read the interview again. Put sentences 1–6 in order.

1 Sue said that she could act better now.
2 Bruno said that the team would win the league.
3 Sue said that she had never been happier.
4 Fiona said that the house was fantastic.
5 Bruno said that he had bought the house.
6 Sue said that she wanted to work in Hollywood again.

A *Hi!* magazine exclusive!

Since their marriage in February, pop star Sue Love and footballer Bruno Hill have been very busy. But last week the famous couple invited our reporter, Fiona, to their new mansion for this exclusive interview.

Fiona Sue, Bruno, the house is fantastic! When did you buy it?
Bruno I bought it last March. It was a present for Sue.
Sue Thank you, darling. Oh, I'm so lucky!
Fiona Are you happy here?
Sue Oh, yes, I've never been happier.
Fiona How many rooms are there?
Bruno Good question. I don't know.
Sue There are forty-seven, and then there are the garages of course!

'I've never been happier.'
'Bruno's the best in the world!'

Fiona Garages?
Sue Yes, we both like cars. We've got seven Rolls Royces.
Fiona Really?
Sue Oh, yes, one for each day of the week.
Fiona Can we talk more about the house? Who chose the colours? They're very strong.
Sue Bruno chose the colours.
Fiona Why orange and purple, Bruno?
Bruno They're my team's colours.
Sue Bruno's in a great team. He's very skilful.
Fiona Do you like football, Sue?
Sue No, but Bruno told me that he was in a great team. Bruno's the best in the world!
Bruno Thank you, darling.
Fiona Will you win the league again this year, Bruno?
Bruno Oh, yes. Of course the team will win the league.
Fiona And what are your plans, Sue? Are you more interested in music or films at the moment?
Sue Oh, I definitely want to work in Hollywood again next year. That's my big ambition.
Fiona Was your first film popular?
Sue No, not exactly. It wasn't a big success.
Bruno People are cruel. Sue's got so much talent. She's the best actress I've ever seen!
Sue Thank you, darling. I can act better now. I've been to classes.
Fiona Have you got any plans to start a family?
Sue No, not yet.
Fiona Really?
Bruno Your readers will know first, I promise!
Fiona Great! Good luck and thanks very much.

Exploring grammar
Reported speech

3 Look at the interview and at exercise 2 again. Complete the table.

Direct speech	Reported speech
Present simple 'The house **is** fantastic.'	**Past simple** Fiona said that the house **was** fantastic.
Past simple 'I (1) ...... the house.'	**Past perfect** Bruno said that he **had bought** the house.
Present perfect 'I**'ve** never **been** happier.'	**Past perfect** Sue said that she (2) ...... never ...... happier.
will 'The team **will** win the league.'	**would** Bruno said that the team (3) ...... win the league.
can 'I (4) ...... act better now.'	**could** Sue said that she could act better now.

GRAMMAR PAGE 123

4 Change the direct speech into reported speech. Change the blue verbs.

Another exclusive:
SUE AND BRUNO SPLIT UP!

'Sue is very happy.' (*Sue's new boyfriend*)
Sue's new boyfriend said that she was very happy.

1 'Sue has found a new love.' (*a friend*)
2 'Bruno will always be a good friend.' (*Sue*)
3 'Bruno isn't angry with Sue.' (*a friend*)
4 'Bruno gave me some great presents.' (*Sue*)
5 'Sue can move to Hollywood now.' (*Bruno*)
6 'Sue won't be successful.' (*a critic*)
7 'Bruno's mother lives with him.' (*Sue*)
8 'We haven't got any Rolls Royces now.' (*Bruno*)

Vocabulary
Fame: adjectives and nouns

5 Complete the table with words from the interview on page 104.

noun	adjective	noun	adjective
fame	*famous*	popularity	(4) ......
luck	(1)	(5)	successful
skill	(2)	(6)	talented
(3)	ambitious		

VOCABULARY PAGE 128, 10.2

6 Choose the correct words. Then listen and check.

Have you got any big (**ambitions**)/ **ambitious**?
1 What's the secret of your **success** / **successful**?
2 Have you been very **luck** / **lucky**?
3 When did you first become **fame** / **famous**?
4 Will you be **popularity** / **popular** for a long time?
5 Who taught you your **skills** / **skilful**?

Speaking

7 Work in pairs. Imagine that you are an interviewer and a famous person. Ask and answer the questions in exercise 6.

Have you got any big ambitions?
Yes, I want to be a really big star...

8 Think of more questions for an interview.

Have you got a mansion?
What colour is your Ferrari?

Finished?

Write about your partner. Use reported speech.
Kim is ambitious. She said that she wanted to be a really big star.

10c Good news

Listening

1 Read the information about a radio programme. Do you read newspapers or watch the news on TV? Why / why not?

SATURDAY 4 January
Voice of the Young

Teenagers discuss how to make the world a better place. This week, student Sandra Deeble suggests ways of improving newspapers.

2 Listen to the interview. Which topics do the people mention?
- ecology
- crime
- entertainment
- disasters
- science
- war
- economics
- business
- politics
- computers

3 Read the opinions. Does Sandra agree or disagree with them? Listen to the interview again and check your answers.
1 Ecology is a boring subject.
2 Newspapers are depressing.
3 It's important to know the news.
4 Photos in newspapers show too much violence.
5 There's a lot of information for young people in newspapers.

Speaking

4 Look at the headline and the picture. Imagine that you are going to interview the boy. Think of ten questions to ask. Use some of the words in the box.

> When ...? How ...? Who ...? Why ...?
> How many ...? What ...? Did ...?
> How long ...?

1 When did this happen?

Boy in dramatic cable car rescue

5 Work in pairs. Ask and answer the questions from exercise 4.

A: When did this happen?
B: It happened last August when I was on holiday with my family.

106

Writing

A news story: summary sentences

6 Complete the newspaper article with the words in the box.

> insects   road   farm   experts

Bees on the move

The accident happened at about 4.20 p.m. on a dangerous section of the road. Witnesses said the weather was bad and the driver crashed after he had lost control of his vehicle. The lorry was carrying 450 beehives to a (1)_____ in the Frambury area. Each of the hives contained approximately 40,000 bees, and police had to close the A235 road when the (2)_____ became a problem for other drivers.

A police officer at the scene said, 'I have never seen so many bees in my life.' Two bee experts were called to help with the situation. One of the (3)_____, Dave Jones, explained, 'We use smoke to make the bees sleep. It doesn't kill them, but it makes them less dangerous.'

The (4)_____ was opened again five hours later, after the experts had moved all of the bees.

7 Choose the best summary sentence to introduce the newspaper story.

a There was an accident yesterday and some bees attacked drivers when they escaped from a lorry.

b Police closed the A235 road in Frambury yesterday, after a lorry carrying millions of bees crashed in bad weather conditions.

c Bees are interesting insects and there were a lot of them in Frambury yesterday when they escaped after an accident.

8 Read the notes and write a summary sentence for each news story.

1 What happened? — Police arrested two men.
   Where? — In Oxford.
   When? — This morning.
   Why? — They saw them stealing from a shop.

2 What happened? — Three people were taken to hospital.
   Where? — In Aspen, Colorado.
   When? — Last night.
   Why? — They had an accident while they were skiing.

9 Write a newspaper report about the cable car drama in exercise 4. Use this plan.

Paragraph 1: A summary sentence.

Paragraph 2: Details of the event and some interesting information.

Paragraph 3: Quotations from one or two people.

Paragraph 4: A conclusion – the situation now.

Finished?

Invent a funny or a happy news story. Use the names of your friends.

Samuel and Alex were surprised yesterday when they received a phone call from Manchester United Football Club.

Unit 10 *News and views*

Progress Check 10

News topics

1 Match the news in sentences 1–6 with the topics in the box.

> lifestyle   science and medicine
> culture and entertainment   ecology
> politics   economics and business

1 The government will not meet again until next week.

2 More than a million people have already bought the *Lord of the Rings* DVD.

3 Genetic research will help to produce new drugs.

4 You can buy this fabulous sofa in three different colours.

5 Petrol prices increased again last week.

6 The new recycling bins will help people to think more about the environment.

Fame: adjectives and nouns

2 Complete the words in the questions. Then write answers.

1 Are your friends tal _ _ _ _ _ ?
2 Who is the most skil _ _ _ player in the team?
3 Which is more important, money or popul _ _ _ _ _ ?
4 What problems do fam _ _ _ people have?
5 Do you feel luc _ _ today?

Past perfect

3 Rewrite the sentences. Use the past perfect and *because*.

She lost her car keys. She phoned a taxi.

She phoned a taxi because she had lost her car keys.

1 She wrote three books. She was famous.
2 His team won the league. He was happy.
3 She asked for a new house. He bought her the mansion.
4 Robert didn't win the lottery. He was sad.
5 She saw a robbery. She called the police.

Reported speech

4 Rewrite the sentences. Use reported speech.

'Humans are my favourite food,' said the bear.

The bear said that humans were his favourite food.

1 'I've eaten in all the best rivers,' said the crocodile.

2 'My girlfriend is a beginner,' said the frog.

3 'I'll be a good husband,' said the snake.

4 'I met Santa Claus once,' said the reindeer.

5 'You'll be a star one day,' said the mouse.

108

The World of English 5

North Street (pages 110 and 111)

Revision: reported speech, past passive, modal verbs

Function: Making offers and requests

1 Who makes the invitations for the party?

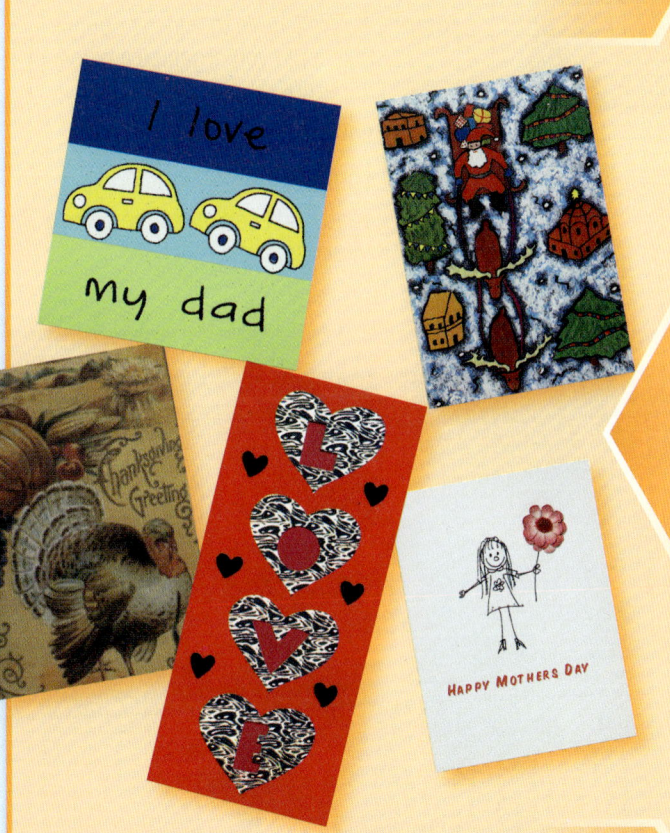

Culture File (pages 112 and 113)

Topic: Special days

2 When is Thanksgiving?

The Story of Pop (page 114)

Artist: Sister Sledge
Type of music: Disco
Song: We are family

3 When did disco first become popular?

North Street

Let's have a party!

1

Maxine What are we going to do for the end of term? Ms Rossi said that she wanted to have a party.
Josie I know – let's have a fancy dress party.
Rick Good idea! Who shall we invite?
Maxine People from our class, and some teachers, I suppose.

2

Josie OK. We'll have to think about this. Max, could you organize a place for the party?
Maxine Yeah, no problem.
Rick I'll bring the music.
Josie Great! And I can make the invitations.
Rick Excellent!

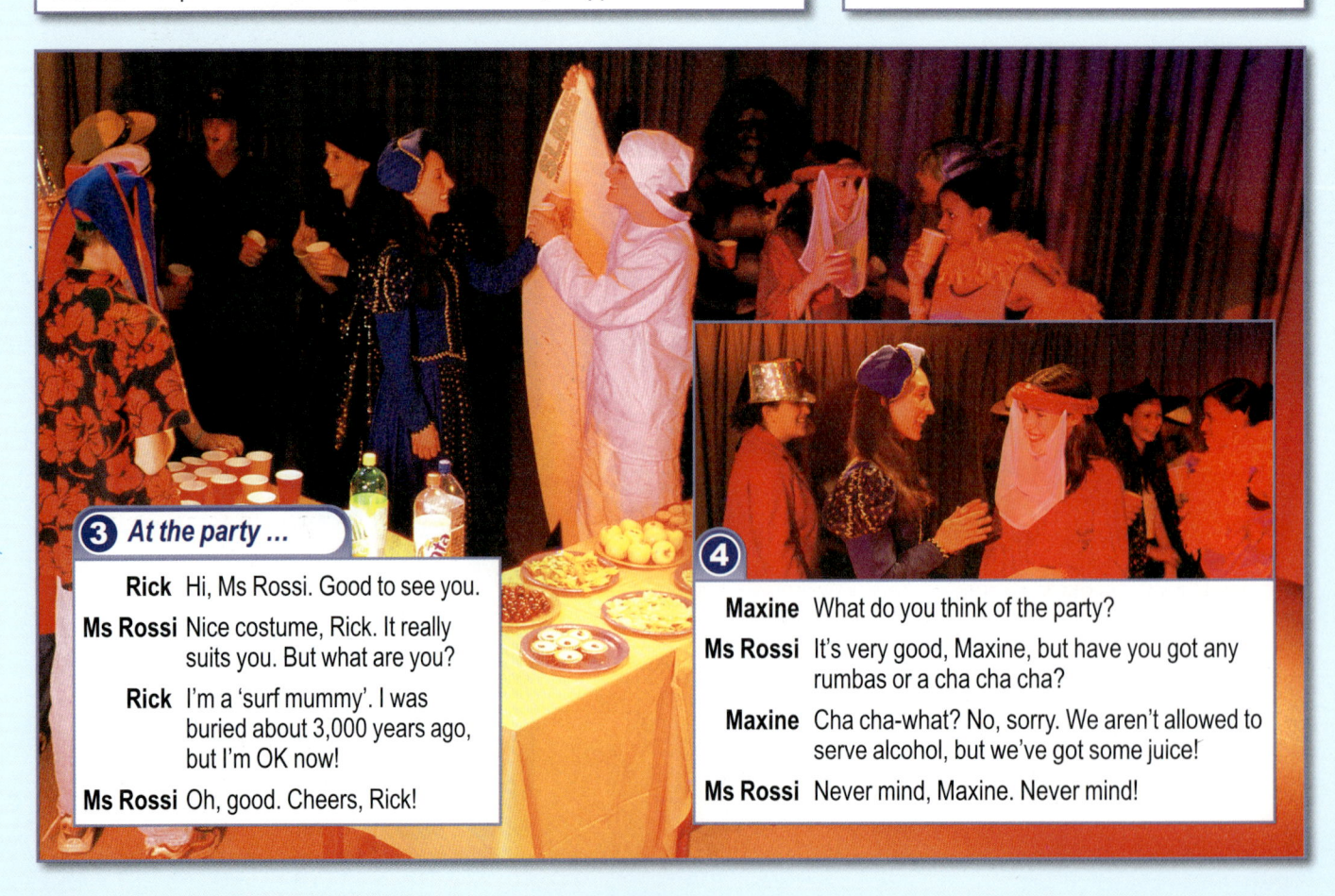

3 At the party …

Rick Hi, Ms Rossi. Good to see you.
Ms Rossi Nice costume, Rick. It really suits you. But what are you?
Rick I'm a 'surf mummy'. I was buried about 3,000 years ago, but I'm OK now!
Ms Rossi Oh, good. Cheers, Rick!

4

Maxine What do you think of the party?
Ms Rossi It's very good, Maxine, but have you got any rumbas or a cha cha cha?
Maxine Cha cha-what? No, sorry. We aren't allowed to serve alcohol, but we've got some juice!
Ms Rossi Never mind, Maxine. Never mind!

Reading

1 Read and listen to North Street. Then answer the questions.

1. What type of party does Josie suggest?
2. Who must they invite?
3. Who is going to organize the music for the party?
4. What happened to Rick 3,000 years ago?
5. What did Maxine say about alcohol?

Useful expressions

2 Find the expressions in the story. Then check their meaning.

1. Good to see you.
2. It really suits you.
3. Cheers, Rick!
4. Never mind!

Dialogue

Making offers and requests

3 Look at this extract from North Street. Listen and repeat. Concentrate on your rhythm and intonation.

A: OK. We'll have to think about this. Max, could you organize a place for the party?
B: Yeah, no problem.
C: I'll bring the music.
A: Great! And I can make the invitations.
C: Excellent!

4 Imagine that you are organizing one of these activities. Make a list of things to do.

repainting the classroom
 1 buy the paint
 2 cover the desks and chairs
 3 find people to help

1. a school trip
2. a surprise birthday barbecue for a friend
3. a fashion show

5 In groups of three, discuss your lists from exercise 4. Use exercise 3 as a model. Substitute the blue words to form your own dialogues.

A: OK. We'll have to think about this. Andrew, could you buy the paint?
B: Yeah, no problem.
C: I'll cover the desks and chairs.
A: Great! And I can find people to help.
C: Excellent!

The World of English 5   **111**

Culture File 5

Special days

🇬🇧 🇺🇸

1 Look at the pictures. What can you see? Use some of the words in the box.

> cards   decorations   candles   turkey
> costumes   lights   Christmas tree
> stockings   fireworks   presents

2 Look at the cards and dates of the celebrations. Answer the questions.

1 Do you celebrate all of these things?
2 Are the dates the same in your country?
3 What other things do you celebrate?
4 When do you have your school holidays?

Happy days!

Father's Day:
third Sunday in June (UK and USA)

Mrs Sonora Dodd of Washington, USA, first had the idea of a father's day in 1909. Her father raised his six children alone after his wife died. His daughter wanted to say 'thank you' to him.

Mother's Day:
fourth Sunday in Lent (UK)

Mother's Day has got different origins in different countries. In the seventeenth century in England, a lot of servants worked in the houses of rich people. Servants had a special holiday called 'Mothering Sunday', when they went home and visited their families.

3 Read the texts and write the names of celebrations 1–5.

> A new tradition – Father's Day
> A Roman festival for winter – (**1**) ......
> A harvest festival – (**2**) ......
> An old English tradition – Mothering (**3**) ......
> A Roman festival for spring – (**4**) ......
> A combination of pagan and Christian festivals – Christmas and (**5**) ......

Christmas:
25th December (UK and USA)
Before the birth of Jesus Christ, people celebrated winter festivals. In some of these pagan festivals people decorated their houses. In the Roman festival of Saturnalia, in December, people gave presents to their relatives and to the poor.
When Christmas replaced these festivals, some of these old pagan traditions continued.

Thanksgiving:
fourth Thursday in November (USA)
Thanksgiving is a harvest festival in the USA and Canada. The first Europeans in these countries gave thanks for their harvests, and the celebration became an official national holiday.

Saint Valentine's Day:
14th February (UK and USA)
The Romans had a spring festival called Lupercalia on 15th February, when young people chose partners. This pagan celebration later became a Christian festival in honour of Saint Valentine. Valentine was a priest, and he organized secret Christian weddings. Because of this the Romans executed him on 14th February 273.

4 Read the texts again and answer the questions.
1. Why did Mrs Dodd want to thank her father?
2. Has Mother's Day got the same history in every country?
3. What pagan traditions are part of our Christmas celebrations?
4. Who celebrated the first thanksgivings?
5. What did young people do in Lupercalia?
6. Why did the Romans execute Saint Valentine?

5 Read the text and look at the pictures. Discuss the questions and then listen and check.
1. What is the 'New World'?
2. Why do you think that life was hard for the Pilgrims?

The Thanksgiving story
In 1621 a group of people travelled from England to the 'New World'. When they arrived they discovered that their new life was very hard.

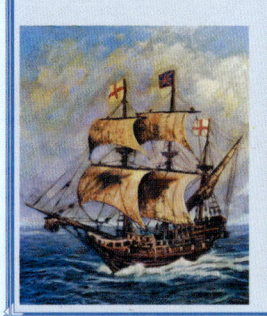

6 Listen again and answer the questions.
1. Was Plymouth a big city in 1620?
2. How many settlers arrived in Plymouth?
3. What did the settlers need in their first year?
4. How many settlers survived the first winter?
5. What did the settlers learn about from the Native American Indians?
6. How did the settlers celebrate their first harvest?

Project
Make a poster about a special day or celebration in your country. Include information about:
- the date.
- the origins of the celebration.
- how people celebrated it in the past.
- how people celebrate it now.

Include photos, drawings or cards.

The World of English 5

The Story of Pop 5

Disco

1 Read and listen. Then answer the questions.

1. What adjectives describe the rhythm of disco music?
2. In which country did the disco explosion begin?
3. How many singers are there in Sister Sledge?
4. Where did the Sledge sisters start singing?
5. What clothes were in fashion in the 1970s?

2 Complete the song with a–d. Then listen and check.

a the things you do   c birds of a feather
b for the future   d we've just begun

Disco

'Discotheques' (discos) first became popular in New York City in the 1970s. Disco DJs played records with a strong, repetitive rhythm. Then radio DJs started to play 'disco', and the disco explosion began! Disco music and disco dancing became incredibly popular in the USA, and then all around the rest of the world.

Sister Sledge

The four Sledge sisters started singing in church when they were very young. When they were older, they decided to form a band. They signed a contract in 1973, but they didn't have a big hit until 1979. *We are family* is one of the most successful disco records in history.

Platform shoes, wide trousers and long hair were popular in the '70s. And today, at the beginning of the 21st century, '70s fashions and music are popular again: people still buy Sister Sledge records!

1970s fashion

We are family

Everyone can see we're together
As we walk on by
And we fly just like (1) ......
I won't tell no lie.
All of the people around us,
They say, 'Can they be that close?'.
Just let me state for the record,
We're giving love in a family dose.

(Chorus)
We are family,
I got all my sisters with me.
We are family,
Get up everybody and sing.

Living life is fun and (2) ......
To get our share of this world's delights.
High hopes we have (3) ......
And our goal's in sight.
No, we don't get depressed.
Here's what we call our golden rule:
Have faith in you and (4) ......
You won't go wrong, oh no,
This is our family jewel.

(Repeat chorus)

Grammar

Unit 1
Present simple

Affirmative	
I	think
you	
he	
she	thinks
it	
we	
you	think
they	

Negative	
I	don't think
you	
he	
she	doesn't think
it	
we	
you	don't think
they	

don't = do not
doesn't = does not

Questions		
Do	I you	think ...?
Does	he she it	think ...?
Do	we you they	think ...?

- We use the present simple to describe routines or repeated actions.
  She always *goes* home at eight o'clock.
  I *cook* dinner every evening.

Spelling: third person singular *s*

- In the third person singular of the present simple, we usually add *s* to the infinitive.
  think   think*s*

- When the verb ends with consonant + *y*, we replace *y* with *ies*.
  copy   cop*ies*

- When the verb ends in *ch*, *ss*, *sh*, *x* or *o*, we add *es*.
  go   go*es*   watch   watch*es*

Present continuous

Affirmative	
I	'm travelling
you	're travelling
he she it	's travelling
we you they	're travelling

Negative	
I	'm not travelling
you	aren't travelling
he she it	isn't travelling
we you they	aren't travelling

Questions		
Am	I	travelling ...?
Are	you	travelling ...?
Is	he she it	travelling ...?
Are	we you they	travelling ...?

Spelling: *ing* form

- We add *ing* to the infinitive of most verbs.
  talk   talk*ing*

- When the verb ends in *e*, we replace *e* with *ing*.
  change   chang*ing*

- When the verb ends in one vowel + one consonant, we double the consonant and add *ing*.
  stop   stop*ping*

Present simple and present continuous

- We use the present simple to describe routines or repeated actions.
  He *gets up* at 7.30 every day.

- We use the present continuous to describe an action that is happening at the moment.
  We*'re watching* TV now.
  NOT: We *watch* TV now.

- We also use the present continuous to talk about arrangements in the future.
  I*'m not going* to the match on Sunday.

Unit 2
Past simple

Affirmative	Negative
I / you / he / she / it / we / you / they danced / saw / stopped	I / you / he / she / it / we / you / they didn't dance / see / stop

didn't = did not

Questions

Did I / you / he / she / it / we / you / they dance …? see …? stop …?

- **The past simple form of regular and irregular verbs is the same for all the persons in the singular and the plural.**
  I *liked* the film. You *liked* the film.
  She *liked* the film.
  I *saw* the film. You *saw* the film.
  She *saw* the film.

- **We use the past simple to describe finished actions in the past.**
  She *danced* a lot yesterday.
  He *won* the competition last year.
  We *didn't go* to bed at midnight.

- **We also use the past simple to describe states in the past.**
  I *felt* terrible yesterday.
  You *weren't* happy last weekend.

Spelling: past simple regular verbs

- **We add *ed* to the infinitive of most verbs.**
  talk   talk*ed*

- **When the verb ends in *e*, we add *d*.**
  change   change*d*

- **When the verb ends in a consonant + *y*, we replace *y* with *ied*.**
  copy   cop*ied*

- **When the verb ends in one vowel + one consonant, we double the consonant and add *ed*.**
  stop   stop*ped*

Past simple irregular verbs

- **Some verbs are irregular. There are no rules for the formation of irregular verbs. You need to learn each verb individually.**
  go   *went*   know   *knew*
  have *had*   see   *saw*

  IRREGULAR VERBS ▸ INSIDE BACK COVER

- **The past simple form of irregular verbs is the same for all the persons in the singular and the plural.**

- **We form the past simple negative and question forms of irregular verbs in the same way as for regular verbs.**
  I *didn't have* dinner   We *didn't go* to Spain.
  Did you *have* dinner?   *Did* they *go* to Spain?

Subject and object questions

- **When a question word asks about an object, we use *do* or *does* in the present simple or *did* in the past simple.**

  Subject   Object
  Tom   saw   someone   yesterday.
  Who   *did*   Tom   *see*   yesterday?

- **When a question word asks about a subject, we don't use *do* or *does* in the present simple or *did* in the past simple. The verb is the same form as in a statement.**

  Subject   Object
  Someone   saw   Tom   yesterday.
  Who   *saw*   Tom   yesterday?

Past continuous

Affirmative	
I	was sleeping
you	were sleeping
he she it	was sleeping
we you they	were sleeping

Negative	
I	wasn't sleeping
you	weren't sleeping
he she it	wasn't sleeping
we you they	weren't sleeping

wasn't = was not
weren't = were not

Questions		
Was	I	sleeping ...?
Were	you	sleeping ...?
Was	he she it	sleeping ...?
Were	we you they	sleeping ...?

- **We use the past continuous to describe the progress of an action in the past.**
  When we arrived, the girls *were talking*.

Past continuous and past simple

- **We use the past continuous to talk about an action in the past that was in progress.**
  What *were* you *doing* at seven o'clock?
  I *was making* the dinner.

- **We use the past simple to describe a completed action in the past.**
  She *went* to school yesterday.

- **We also use the past continuous and past simple together when one action happens in the middle of another, longer action.**
  The robbers *were arguing* when the police *arrived*.

Unit 3
Pronouns: *some...*, *any...* and *every...*

- **We make pronouns by adding *-where*, *-thing* or *-body* to *some*, *any* and *every*.**

somewhere	anywhere	everywhere
something	anything	everything
somebody	anybody	everybody

- **We use *-where* for places.**
  I want to go *somewhere* hot.
  She looked *everywhere* for some new shoes.

- **We use *-thing* for things.**
  Did you buy *anything* to eat?
  Everything is very expensive.

- **We use *-body* for people.**
  I didn't know *anybody* at the party.
  Somebody was knocking on the door.

- **We usually use *some...* in affirmative sentences.**
  There's *something* in my shoe.

- **We usually use *any...* in negative sentences and questions.**
  There isn't *anything* vegetarian on the menu.
  Is there *anywhere* you want to go?

- **But we usually use *some...* in offers and requests.**
  Would you like *something* to eat?
  Can *somebody* close the window, please?

Grammar 117

Countable and uncountable nouns

Countable	Uncountable
a sweet some sweets six sweets	sugar some sugar

- **Countable nouns can be singular or plural.**
  car – cars   *egg – eggs*
- **We can use numbers with countable nouns.**
  one car   *two* cars
- **Uncountable nouns have not got a plural form.**
  money NOT: *moneys*
  water NOT: *waters*
- **We cannot use numbers with uncountable nouns.**
  NOT: *one money*   *two moneys*

Quantity: *a lot of, many, much*

Affirmative

Countable	Uncountable
There are a lot of vitamins in vegetables.	There's a lot of fat in sausages.

Negative

Countable	Uncountable
I haven't got many eggs.	Pasta doesn't contain much fat.

Questions

Countable	Uncountable
How many vitamins are there in this orange?	How much fat is there in this sausage?

- **We use *a lot of* with countable and uncountable nouns in affirmative sentences.**
- **We use *many* with countable nouns in negative sentences and questions.**
- **We use *much* with uncountable nouns in negative sentences and questions.**

(*not*) *enough*, *too much* and *too many*

- *enough* = the necessary quantity
- *not enough* = not sufficient
- **We use (*not*) *enough* after an adjective or adverb.**
  The restaurant is big *enough* for all of us.
  This marmalade isn't sweet *enough*.
- **We use (*not*) *enough* before uncountable and plural countable nouns.**
  Have we got *enough* milk?
  We haven't got *enough* eggs to make a tortilla.
- *too much* / *too many* = more than necessary
- **We use *too much* before uncountable nouns.**
  There's *too much* sugar in my tea.
- **We use *too many* before plural countable nouns.**
  John has bought *too many* pizzas.

Unit 4
Comparative and superlative adjectives

	Adjective	Comparative	Superlative
One syllable ending in a vowel: + r / st	large nice	larger nicer	the largest the nicest
One syllable ending in a consonant: + er / est	bright cheap	brighter cheaper	the brightest the cheapest
Two syllables ending in y: y + ier / iest	friendly heavy	friendlier heavier	the friendliest the heaviest
Two or more syllables: more / the most	beautiful expensive	more beautiful more expensive	the most beautiful the most expensive
Irregular	bad good	worse better	the worst the best

- We use the comparative form of adjectives to compare two things.
  Trainers are *cheaper* than computers.

- We use the superlative form of adjectives to compare three or more things.
  The USA is *the richest* country in the world.

going to and *will*

Affirmative
I	'm	going to be
you	're	going to be
he she it	's	going to be
we you they	're	going to be

Negative
I	'm not	going to be
you	aren't	going to be
he she it	isn't	going to be
we you they	aren't	going to be

'm = am
're = are
's = is

'm = am
aren't = are not
isn't = is not

Questions
Am	I	going to be …?
Are	you	going to be …?
Is	he she it	going to be …?
Are	we you they	going to be …?

Affirmative
| I
you
he
she
it
we
you
they | 'll be |

Negative
| I
you
he
she
it
we
you
they | won't be |

'll = will

won't = will not

- We use *going to* and *will* to talk about the future.

- We use *going to* for plans and intentions.
  I *'m going to go* shopping next week.
  My sister *'s going to be* a shop assistant.

- We use *will* for predictions about the future.
  Everybody *will have* a computer in the future.
  That café probably *won't have* any vegetarian food.

too and (not)… enough

- *too* and *enough* are adverbs.
- *too* = more than necessary.
  This CD costs £15.99 – it's *too* expensive.
- *enough* = the necessary quantity.
  I've got £16.00 – that's *enough* money for a CD.
- *not enough* = not sufficient.
  I've got £8.00 – that is*n't enough* money for a CD.
- **We use *too* before adjectives.**
  The boots are *too* expensive.
- **We use *enough* after adjectives.**
  The boots aren't smart *enough*.

Unit 5
Present perfect

Affirmative	
I / you	've arrived
he / she / it	's arrived
we / you / they	've arrived

Negative	
I / you	haven't arrived
he / she / it	hasn't arrived
we / you / they	haven't arrived

've = have
's = has

haven't = have not
hasn't = has not

Questions		
Have	I / you	arrived …?
Has	he / she / it	arrived …?
Have	we / you / they	arrived …?

- We use the present perfect to talk about experiences in our lives.
  I*'ve been* to America.
  I*'ve* never *read* a book in Italian.

- *Ever* means in your life. The negative form *never* means at no time in our life up to now.
  Have you *ever* driven a car?
  I've *never* been on a plane.

IRREGULAR VERBS INSIDE BACK COVER

Present perfect: *yet* and *already*

- We often use *yet* and *already* with the present perfect.
- We use *yet* at the end of questions and in negative sentences. We use *yet* when we think that an action will happen soon.
  Has he phoned *yet*?
  He hasn't phoned *yet*.
- We use *already* before the past participle when something happened sooner than we expected.
  It's 8 o'clock and they've *already* arrived at school.

Unit 6
Present perfect and past simple

- We use the present perfect to talk about things that have happened up to now. It isn't important when exactly they happened.
  John *has bought* a new surfboard.
- We use the past simple to talk about things that are finished.
  John *bought* a new surfboard last week.

Present perfect: *for* and *since*

- We use the present perfect to talk about things that started in the past and are still happening in the present. We use *for* to say how long a situation has continued.
  I've played in the basketball team *for* ten years.
- We use *since* to say when a situation began.
  I've played in the basketball team *since* 1992.

Present perfect: just

- We use *just* with the present perfect to talk about things that happened a very short time before now.
  Ian has *just* had his first skiing lesson.

- *just* goes after the auxiliary verb.
  NOT: ~~They just have arrived.~~

Unit 7
will and might

Affirmative		Negative	
I you he she it we you they	'll go	I you he she it we you they	won't go

'll = will   won't = will not

Affirmative		Negative	
I you he she it we you they	might stay	I you he she it we you they	might not stay

- We use *will*, *won't*, *might* and *might not* to express our opinions about the future.

- We use *will* and *won't* when we are very sure about our opinions.
  I studied a lot – I *'ll pass* the exam.

- We use *might* and *might not* when when we are not very sure about our opinions.
  She's ill, so she *might not be* at the party.

First conditional

- We use the first conditional to explain the probable consequence of an action.

- We form the first conditional with *If* + present simple, + *will/won't* + infinitive.
  If you *stop* on a black block, you*'ll lose* a life.
  NOT: ~~If you will stop on a black block, you'll lose a life.~~
  If you *don't pick up* the torch, you *won't see* the diamonds.

- We can reverse the order of the clauses. When the *if* clause comes first, there is a comma between the two clauses.
  If you *don't* eat, you*'ll die*.
  You*'ll die if* you *don't eat*.

Second conditional

- We use the second conditional to explain an improbable or hypothetical situation.

- We form the second conditional with *If* + past simple, + *would/wouldn't* + infinitive.
  If I *had* more money, I*'d buy* a car.
  If I *didn't eat* meat, I*'d go* to a vegetarian restaurant.

- We can reverse the order of the clauses. When the *if* clause comes first, there is a comma between the two clauses.
  If I *had* more money, I*'d buy* a car.
  I*'d buy* a car *if* I *had* more money.

Grammar

Unit 8
Permission: can, could and be allowed to

Present		Past	
I you he she it we you they	can can't go out	I you he she it we you they	could couldn't go out

Present	
Affirmative	**Negative**
I 'm allowed to go	I 'm not allowed to go
you 're allowed to go	you aren't allowed to go
he she 's allowed to go it	he she isn't allowed to go it
we you 're allowed to go they	we you aren't allowed to go they

- We use *can*, *could* and *be allowed to* to talk about permission in the present and in the past.
- We use *can* and *could* + verb, without *to*.
  I *couldn't go* out. NOT: I couldn't to go out.
- We use *be allowed to* + verb.
  I *wasn't allowed to go* out.

Obligation: have to and must

- We often use *must* to talk about something that the speaker decides is necessary.
  You *must* pay for the window that you broke.
  We *mustn't* forget to buy Jane a present.
  Must I go? I'd rather stay here.

- We use *have to* when other circumstances make something necessary.
  I *have to* go to the supermarket.
  (= because there isn't any food in the house.)
  Mark *doesn't have to* walk far to school.
  (= because he lives very near.)
  Do you *have to* wear a school uniform?
  (= Is it one of the school rules?)

- *have got to* is a more informal way of saying *have to*. We normally only use it in the present tense.
  I*'ve got to* go home now.
  They *haven't got to* get up early tomorrow.
  Have children *got to* fight in wars in your country?

- *must* has no past or future form. We use *have to* instead.
  We*'ll have to* leave soon.
  He *had to* go into town.

Unit 9
The passive: present simple

Affirmative	**Negative**
I 'm taught	I 'm not taught
you 're taught	you aren't taught
he she 's taught it	he she isn't taught it
we you 're taught they	we you aren't taught they

'm = am
're = are
's = is

The passive: past simple

Affirmative	**Negative**
I was taught	I wasn't taught
you were taught	you weren't taught
he she was taught it	he she wasn't taught it
we you were taught they	we you weren't taught they

IRREGULAR VERBS ▶ INSIDE BACK COVER

The passive (present and past simple)

- We form the present and past simple passive with the correct present simple or past simple form of *be* + past participle.

- We use the passive when we want to emphasize the action and not the 'agent' (the person or the thing that does the action). Compare the active and passive sentences.
  Active: They *make* CDs in Japan.
  Passive: CDs *are made* in Japan.
  Active: People *used* shells for money.
  Passive: Shells *were used* for money.

by

- We use *by* when we want to mention the agent.
  Active: Baird invented TV in 1924.
  Passive: TV was invented *by* Baird in 1924.

Unit 10
Past perfect

Affirmative			Negative	
I you he she it we you they	'd had	seen	I you he she it we you they	hadn't seen

'd = had

IRREGULAR VERBS INSIDE BACK COVER

- We form the past perfect with *had* or *hadn't* + past participle.

- We use the past perfect to talk about an action in the past, which happened before another action in the past.
  When he *'d finished* his homework, he went out.
  OR
  He went out when he *'d finished* his homework.
  (First action: he finished his homework. Second action: he went out.)

Pronunciation: *ed* endings

- *ed* is pronounced /ɪd/ when the verb ends in /t/ or /d/.
  wanted, visited

- *ed* is pronounced /d/ when the verb ends in a vowel or voiced consonant.
  died, rescued

- *ed* is pronounced /t/ when the verb ends in an unvoiced consonant.
  helped, worked

Reported speech

Direct speech	Reported speech
Present simple 'It **looks** great!' →	**Past simple** He said that it **looked** great.
Past simple 'I **saw** the film.' →	**Past perfect** She said that she**'d seen** the film.
Present perfect 'He**'s seen** us.' →	**Past perfect** I said that he**'d seen** us.
will 'This **will** help.' →	**would** He said that this **would** help.
can 'It **can't** see us.' →	**could** She said that it **couldn't** see us.

- We use reported speech to report what people have said.

Grammar **123**

Vocabulary

Unit 1
1.1 Adjectives describing personality
active /ˈæktɪv/
aggressive /əˈgresɪv/
calm /kɑ:m/
cheeky /ˈtʃi:ki/
cheerful /ˈtʃɪəfl/
confident /ˈkɒnfɪdənt/
dishonest /dɪsˈɒnɪst/
friendly /ˈfrendli/
honest /ˈɒnɪst/
lazy /ˈleɪzi/
moody /ˈmu:di/
quiet /ˈkwaɪət/
shy /ʃaɪ/
talkative /ˈtɔ:kətɪv/
unfriendly /ʌnˈfrendli/

1.2 Adverbs of manner
angrily /ˈæŋgrəli/
badly /ˈbædli/
calmly /ˈkɑ:mli/
happily /ˈhæpəli/
loudly /ˈlaʊdli/
quickly /ˈkwɪkli/
quietly /ˈkwaɪətli/
sadly /ˈsædli/
slowly /ˈsləʊli/
well /wel/

1.3 Nouns
action /ˈækʃn/
analysis /əˈnæləsɪs/
appearance /əˈpɪərəns/
body language /ˈbɒdi læŋgwɪdʒ/
chalk /tʃɔ:k/
character /ˈkærəktə(r)/
cheese /tʃi:z/
emotion /ɪˈməʊʃn/
energy /ˈenədʒi/
experience /ɪkˈspɪəriəns/
expert /ˈekspɜ:t/
feelings /ˈfi:lɪŋz/
finger /ˈfɪŋgə(r)/
gene /dʒi:n/
gesture /ˈdʒestʃə(r)/
graphology /græˈfɒlədʒi/
group /gru:p/
handwriting /ˈhændraɪtɪŋ/
image /ˈɪmɪdʒ/
mate /meɪt/
mix /mɪks/
palm /pɑ:m/
per cent /pə ˈsent/
temperament /ˈtemprəmənt/
truth /tru:θ/

1.4 Verbs
become /bɪˈkʌm/
blush /blʌʃ/
change /tʃeɪndʒ/
control /kənˈtrəʊl/
copy /ˈkɒpi/
influence /ˈɪnfluəns/
joke /dʒəʊk/
laugh /lɑ:f/
mimic /ˈmɪmɪk/
point /pɔɪnt/
relax /rɪˈlæks/
show /ʃəʊ/
tell /tel/

1.5 Other adjectives
bossy /ˈbɒsi/
comfortable /ˈkʌmftəbl/
defensive /dɪˈfensɪv/
energetic /enəˈdʒetɪk/
extrovert /ˈekstrəvɜ:t/
similar /ˈsɪmələ(r)/

Unit 2
2.1 Crimes
drug dealing /ˈdrʌg di:lɪŋ/
kidnapping /ˈkɪdnæpɪŋ/
murder /ˈmɜ:də(r)/
pickpocketing /ˈpɪkpɒkɪtɪŋ/
robbery /ˈrɒbəri/
smuggling /ˈsmʌglɪŋ/
speeding /ˈspi:dɪŋ/
vandalism /ˈvændəlɪzm/

2.2 Crime stories: verbs
arrest /əˈrest/
confess /kənˈfes/
discover /dɪˈskʌvə(r)/
escape /ɪˈskeɪp/
find /faɪnd/
hide /haɪd/
plan /plæn/
shoot /ʃu:t/
steal /sti:l/
suspect /səˈspekt/

2.3 Criminals
drug dealer /ˈdrʌg di:lə(r)/
kidnapper /ˈkɪdnæpə(r)/
murderer /ˈmɜ:dərə(r)/
robber /ˈrɒbə(r)/
smuggler /ˈsmʌglə(r)/

2.4 Other nouns
beer /bɪə(r)/
businessman /ˈbɪznɪsmən/
chemical /ˈkemɪkl/
chemistry /ˈkeməstri/
clue /klu:/
confession /kənˈfeʃn/
conversation /kɒnvəˈseɪʃn/
cook /kʊk/
customer /ˈkʌstəmə(r)/
detective /dɪˈtektɪv/
diamond /ˈdaɪəmənd/
DVD player /di: vi: ˈdi: pleɪə(r)/
helmet /ˈhelmɪt/
hypnotist /ˈhɪpnətɪst/
identity /aɪˈdentəti/
manager /ˈmænɪdʒə(r)/
necklace /ˈnekləs/
plastic bag /ˈplæstɪk bæg/
poison /ˈpɔɪzn/
police /pəˈli:s/
prison /ˈprɪzn/
prisoner /ˈprɪznə(r)/
punishment /ˈpʌnɪʃmənt/
snake /sneɪk/
victim /ˈvɪktɪm/

2.5 Other verbs
accuse /əˈkju:z/
argue /ˈɑ:gju:/
borrow /ˈbɒrəʊ/
break /breɪk/
carry /ˈkæri/
commit /kəˈmɪt/
hypnotize /ˈhɪpnətaɪz/
investigate /ɪnˈvestɪgeɪt/
record /rɪˈkɔ:d/
remember /rɪˈmembə(r)/

2.6 Adjectives
cruel /krʊəl/
good-looking /gʊd ˈlʊkɪŋ/
greedy /ˈgri:di/
illegal /ɪˈli:gl/
jealous /ˈdʒeləs/
mean /mi:n/
ugly /ˈʌgli/

World of English 1
Useful expressions
Hang on a second. /hæŋ ɒn ə ˈsekənd/
Nice to meet you. /naɪs tə mi:t ju/
See you later. /si: ju: ˈleɪtə(r)/
We'll see. /wi:əl ˈsi:/

International English
bilingual /baɪˈlɪŋgwəl/
colonize /ˈkɒlənaɪz/
communicate /kəˈmju:nɪkeɪt/
internet /ˈɪntənet/
native speaker /neɪtɪv ˈspi:kə(r)/
population /pɒpjəˈleɪʃn/

Unit 3

3.1 Food
egg /eg/
ham /hæm/
mushroom /ˈmʌʃruːm/
olive /ˈɒlɪv/
onion /ˈʌnjən/
pepper /ˈpepə(r)/
pineapple /ˈpaɪnæpl/
pizza /ˈpiːtsə/
prawn /prɔːn/
sweetcorn /ˈswiːtkɔːn/
tuna /ˈtjuːnə/

3.2 Preparing food: verbs and adjectives
bake /beɪk/
baked /beɪkt/
boil /bɔɪl/
boiled /bɔɪld/
freeze /friːz/
fried /fraɪd/
frozen /ˈfrəʊzn/
fry /fraɪ/
grill /grɪl/
grilled /grɪld/
roast /rəʊst/

3.3 Other nouns
Aborigine /æbəˈrɪdʒəni/
ant /ænt/
atmosphere /ˈætməsfɪə(r)/
café /ˈkæfeɪ/
chocolate /ˈtʃɒklət/
cholesterol /kəˈlestərɒl/
cricket /ˈkrɪkɪt/
delicacy /ˈdelɪkəsi/
dessert /dɪˈzɜːt/
diet /ˈdaɪət/
fat /fæt/
fibre /ˈfaɪbə(r)/
fly /flaɪ/
grasshopper /ˈgrɑːshɒpə(r)/
ingredient /ɪnˈgriːdiənt/
insect /ˈɪnsekt/
main course /meɪn kɔːs/
menu /ˈmenjuː/
omelette /ˈɒmlət/
oven /ˈʌvn/
price /praɪs/
protein /ˈprəʊtiːn/
recipe /ˈresəpi/
restaurant /ˈrestrɒnt/
salad /ˈsæləd/
sausage /ˈsɒsɪdʒ/
service /ˈsɜːvɪs/
snack /snæk/
souvenir /suːvəˈnɪə(r)/
staff /stɑːf/
sugar /ˈʃʊgə(r)/
sweet tooth /swiːt tuːθ/
taste /teɪst/
vegetable /ˈvedʒtəbl/
vitamin /ˈvɪtəmɪn/

3.4 Other verbs
contain /kənˈteɪn/
peel /piːl/
produce /prəˈdjuːs/
stir /stɜː(r)/

3.5 Other adjectives
delicious /dɪˈlɪʃəs/
excellent /ˈeksələnt/
fresh /freʃ/
healthy /ˈhelθi/
interesting /ˈɪntrəstɪŋ/
strange /streɪndʒ/
theme /θiːm/
vegetarian /vedʒɪˈteəriən/

Unit 4

4.1 Shopping
advert /ˈædvɜːt/
customer /ˈkʌstəmə(r)/
logo /ˈləʊgəʊ/
price /praɪs/
shelf /ʃelf/
shop assistant /ˈʃɒp əˌsɪstənt/
slogan /ˈsləʊgən/
special offer /speʃl ˈɒfə(r)/

4.2 Adjectives
big /bɪg/
bright /braɪt/
cheap /tʃiːp/
dangerous /ˈdeɪndʒərəs/
dull /dʌl/
expensive /ɪkˈspensɪv/
fashionable /ˈfæʃnəbl/
unfashionable /ʌnˈfæʃnəbl/
fast /fɑːst/
heavy /ˈhevi/
light /laɪt/
safe /seɪf/
slow /sləʊ/
small /smɔːl/

4.3 Other nouns
advertising /ˈædvətaɪzɪŋ/
angel /ˈeɪndʒl/
boots /buːts/
company /ˈkʌmpəni/
cow /kaʊ/
design /dɪˈzaɪn/
dream /driːm/
exit /ˈegzɪt/
eye level /ˈaɪ levl/
farmer /ˈfɑːmə(r)/
feather /ˈfeðə(r)/
field /fiːld/
ice /aɪs/
image /ˈɪmɪdʒ/
lightning /ˈlaɪtnɪŋ/
motorway /ˈməʊtəweɪ/
paradise /ˈpærədaɪs/
perfume /ˈpɜːfjuːm/
place /pleɪs/
product /ˈprɒdʌkt/
score /skɔː(r)/
shoe /ʃuː/
side /saɪd/
steel /stiːl/
symbol /ˈsɪmbl/
trainer /ˈtreɪnə(r)/
wind /wɪnd/

4.4 Verbs
advertise /ˈædvətaɪz/
appear /əˈpɪə(r)/
buy /baɪ/
receive /rɪˈsiːv/
sell /sel/

4.5 Other adjectives
attractive /əˈtræktɪv/
horrible /ˈhɒrəbl/
imaginative /ɪˈmædʒɪnətɪv/
important /ɪmˈpɔːtənt/
unusual /ʌnˈjuːʒʊəl/

World of English 2

Useful expressions
Sorry I'm late. /ˈsɒri aɪm leɪt/
Sweet dreams. /swiːt driːmz/
That's enough. /ðæts ɪˈnʌf/
That's very kind of you. /ðæts ˈveri kaɪnd əv juː/

Multiracial societies
accent /ˈæksənt/
Christian /ˈkrɪstʃən/
church /tʃɜːtʃ/
Hindu /ˈhɪnduː, hɪnˈduː/
immigrant /ˈɪmɪgrənt/
Islam /ˈɪzlɑːm, ɪzˈlɑːm/
mosque /mɒsk/
multicultural /mʌltiˈkʌltʃərəl/
Muslim /ˈmʊzlɪm/
race /reɪs/
religion /rɪˈlɪdʒən/
temple /ˈtempl/

Unit 5

5.1 Jobs
bank manager /'bæŋk mænɪdʒə(r)/
basketball player /'bɑːskɪtbɔːl pleɪə(r)/
beauty consultant /'bjuːti kənsʌltənt/
bus driver /'bʌs draɪvə(r)/
civil servant /sɪvɪl 'sɜːvənt/
computer programmer /kəmpjuːtə 'prəʊgræmə(r)/
construction worker /kən'strʌkʃn wɜːkə(r)/
electrical engineer /ɪlektrɪkl endʒɪ'nɪə(r)/
Geography teacher /dʒɪ'ɒgrəfi tiːtʃə(r)/
motorbike mechanic /'məʊtəbaɪk məkænɪk/

5.2 Adjectives: qualities for jobs
ambitious /æm'bɪʃʌs/
communicative /kəm'juːnɪkətɪv/
competitive /kəm'petətɪv/
creative /kriː'eɪtɪv/
experienced /eks'pɪəriənst/
fit /fɪt/
mature /mə'tʃʊə(r)/
organized /'ɔːgənaɪzd/
practical /'præktɪkl/
reliable /rɪ'laɪəbl/

5.3 Other nouns
accident /'æksɪdənt/
applicant /'æplɪkənt/
application form /æplɪ'keɪʃn fɔːm/
au pair /əʊ 'peə(r)/
avalanche /'ævəlɑːntʃ/
benefit /'benəfɪt/
boss /bɒs/
child labour /tʃaɪld leɪbə(r)/
colleague /'kɒliːg/
demo tape /'deməʊ teɪp/
factory /'fæktri/
gig /gɪg/
holiday /'hɒlɪdeɪ/
knowledge /'nɒlɪdʒ/
ladder /'lædə(r)/
pay rise /'peɪ raɪz/
qualification /kwɒlɪfɪ'keɪʃn/
salary /'sæləri/
school-leaver /'skuːl liːvə(r)/
skill /skɪl/
snowboarder /'snəʊbɔːdə(r)/
snowboarding /'snəʊbɔːdɪŋ/
success /sək'ses/
the Rockies /ðə 'rɒkiːz/
tip /tɪp/
vacancy /'veɪkənsi/
web page designer /'web peɪdʒ dɪzaɪnə(r)/

5.4 Other verbs
accept /ə'ksept/
annoy /ə'nɔɪ/
apply /ə'plaɪ/
impress /ɪm'pres/

5.5 Other adjectives
agricultural /'ægrɪkʌltʃə(r)/
basic /'beɪsɪk/
following /'fɒləʊɪŋ/
formal /'fɔːml/
part-time /'pɑːt taɪm/
hard-working /hɑːd 'wɜːkɪŋ/
trainee /treɪ'niː/
racing /'reɪsɪŋ/
wanted /'wɒntɪd/

Unit 6

6.1 Sports
canoeing /kə'nuːɪŋ/
climbing /'klaɪmɪŋ/
diving /'daɪvɪŋ/
parachuting /'pærəʃuːtɪŋ/
sailing /'seɪlɪŋ/
skateboarding /'skeɪtbɔːdɪŋ/
skating /'skeɪtɪŋ/
skiing /'skiːɪŋ/
snowboarding /'snəʊbɔːdɪŋ/
surfing /'sɜːfɪŋ/

6.2 Sports equipment
bodyboard /'bɒdibɔːd/
goggles /'gɒglz/
helmet /'helmɪt/
(inline) skate /('ɪnlaɪn) skeɪt/
mask /mɑːsk/
oxygen cylinder /'ɒksɪdʒən sɪlɪndə(r)/
parachute /'pærəʃuːt/
skateboard /'skeɪtbɔːd/
surfboard /'sɜːfbɔːd/
wetsuit /'wetsuːt/

6.3 Other nouns
accident /'æksɪdənt/
agony /'ægəni/
air-surfing /'eə sɜːfɪŋ/
altitude /'æltɪtjuːd/
body /'bɒdi/
climber /'klaɪmə(r)/
compass /'kʌmpəs/
Death Zone /'deθ zəʊn/
diver /'daɪvə(r)/
expedition /ekspə'dɪʃn/
explorer /ɪk'splɔːrə(r)/
kilometre /'kɪləmiːtə(r), kɪ'lɒmɪtə(r)/
knife /naɪf/
mountain /'maʊntɪn/
risk /rɪsk/
safety /'seɪfti/
shark /ʃɑːk/
skysurfer /'skaɪsɜːfə(r)/
step /step/
summit /'sʌmɪt/
wind /wɪnd/

6.4 Verbs
breathe /briːð/
cause /kɔːz/
check /tʃek/
climb /klaɪm/
conquer /'kɒŋkə(r)/
disagree /dɪsə'griː/
exist /ɪg'zɪst/
jump /dʒʌmp/
move /muːv/
reach /riːtʃ/
share /ʃeə(r)/
survive /sə'vaɪv/

6.5 Adjectives
continual /kən'tɪnjʊəl/
extreme /ɪk'striːm/
second-hand /'sekənd hænd/
tired /'taɪəd/
unpopular /ʌn'pɒpjələ(r)/

World of English 3

Useful expressions
He's a real pain. /hiːz ə rɪəl peɪn/
He's got a nerve. /hiːz gɒt ə nɜːv/
It doesn't matter. /ɪt 'dʌznt 'mætə(r)/
Nice one! /naɪs wʌn/

Teenage problems
bullying /'bʊliɪŋ/
depression /dɪ'preʃn/
eating problems /'iːtɪŋ prɒbləmz/
ID card /aɪ'diː kɑːd/
police patrol /pə'liːs pə'trəʊl/
racism /'reɪsɪzm/
relationship /rɪ'leɪʃnʃɪp/
security guard /sɪ'kjʊərɪti gɑːd/
sniffer dog /snɪfə dɒg/
stress /stres/
surveillance camera /sə'veɪləns 'kæmrə/

Unit 7

7.1 Computers
joystick /ˈdʒɔɪstɪk/
keyboard /ˈkiːbɔːd/
mat /mæt/
monitor /ˈmɒnɪtə(r)/
mouse /maʊs/
printer /ˈprɪntə(r)/
scanner /ˈskænə(r)/
screen /skriːn/
speaker /ˈspiːkə(r)/
webcam /ˈwebkæm/

7.2 Movement: verbs + prepositions
across /əˈkrɒs/
climb /klaɪm/
down /daʊn/
go /gəʊ/
jump /dʒʌmp/
on /ɒn/
run /rʌn/
swim /swɪm/
through /θruː/
walk /wɔːk/

7.3 The internet
chat room /ˈtʃæt ruːm/
cyberpal /ˈsaɪbəpæl/
download /ˈdaʊnləʊd/
e-mail /ˈiːmeɪl/
online /ɒnˈlaɪn/
search engine /ˈsɜːtʃ endʒɪn/
virus /ˈvaɪrəs/
website /ˈwebsaɪt/

7.4 Other nouns
adventure /ədˈventʃə(r)/
archive /ˈɑːkaɪv/
article /ˈɑːtɪkl/
block /blɒk/
castle /ˈkɑːsl/
chamber /ˈtʃeɪmbə(r)/
cup /kʌp/
domain /dəˈmeɪn/
gate /geɪt/
guard /gɑːd/
key /kiː/
lizard /ˈlɪzəd/
master /ˈmɑːstə(r)/
mini-mobile /ˌmɪni ˈməʊbaɪl/
MP3 /em piː ˈθriː/
review /rɪˈvjuː/
ring /rɪŋ/
river /ˈrɪvə(r)/
sword /sɔːd/
torch /tɔːtʃ/
tower /ˈtaʊə(r)/
troll /trɒl/
trophy /ˈtrəʊfi/
tunnel /ˈtʌnl/

7.5 Other verbs
connect /kəˈnekt/
lose /luːz/
pick up /pɪk ˈʌp/
transfer /trænsˈfɜː(r)/

7.6 Adjectives
computerized /kəmˈpjuːtəraɪzd/
educational /ˌedʒʊˈkeɪʃənl/
gold /gəʊld/
invisible /ɪnˈvɪzəbl/
magic /ˈmædʒɪk/
real /ˈriːəl/
virtual /ˈvɜːtʃʊəl/

Unit 8

8.1 Legal and illegal
alcohol /ˈælkəhɒl/
bullying /ˈbʊliɪŋ/
drug /drʌg/
gang /gæŋ/
graffiti /grəˈfiːti/
gun /gʌn/
hunting /ˈhʌntɪŋ/
protest /ˈprəʊtest/
slavery /ˈsleɪvəri/
smoking /ˈsməʊkɪŋ/

8.2 Household tasks and objects
clean the floor /kliːn ðə ˈflɔː(r)/
coffee machine/maker /ˈkɒfi məˌʃiːn, ˌmeɪkə(r)/
cook /kʊk/
cooker /ˈkʊkə/
mop /mɒp/
dishwasher /ˈdɪʃwɒʃə(r)/
iron /ˈaɪən/
iron your clothes /aɪən jɔː ˈkləʊðz/
make coffee /meɪk ˈkɒfi/
wash the dishes /wɒʃ ðə ˈdɪʃɪz/
wash your clothes /wɒʃ jɔː ˈkləʊðz/
washing machine /ˈwɒʃɪŋ məˌʃiːn/

8.3 Other nouns
attitude /ˈætɪtjuːd/
battle /ˈbætl/
bully /ˈbʊli/
chewing gum /ˈtʃuːɪŋ gʌm/
consumption /kənˈsʌmpʃn/
discipline /ˈdɪsəplɪn/
inequality /ˌɪnɪˈkwɒləti/
law /lɔː/
monarch /ˈmɒnək/
percentage /pəˈsentɪdʒ/
prohibition /ˌprəʊɪˈbɪʃn/
rule /ruːl/
suffragette /ˌsʌfrəˈdʒet/
sultan /ˈsʌltən/
tattoo /təˈtuː/
tobacco /təˈbækəʊ/
tutor /ˈtjuːtə(r)/
TV licence /tiː ˈviː laɪsəns/
uniform /ˈjuːnɪfɔːm/
weapon /ˈwepən/

8.4 Verbs
allow /əˈlaʊ/
apologize /əˈpɒlədʒaɪz/
ban /bæn/
chew /tʃuː/
dye /daɪ/
execute /ˈeksɪkjuːt/
respect /rɪˈspekt/
vote /vəʊt/

8.5 Adjectives
anti-social /ˌænti ˈsəʊʃl/
banned /bænd/
cruel /kruːəl/
delighted /dɪˈlaɪtɪd/
fair /feə(r)/
female /ˈfiːmeɪl/
firm /fɜːm/
guilty /ˈgɪlti/
responsible /rɪˈspɒnsəbl/
soft /sɒft/
strict /strɪkt/

8.6 Expressing contrast
although /ɔːlˈðəʊ/
but /bʌt, bət/
however /haʊˈevə(r)/
on the other hand /ɒn ði ˈʌðə hænd/

World of English 4

Useful expressions
He's not my type. /hiːz nɒt maɪ taɪp/
I'm completely broke. /aɪm kəmpliːtli ˈbrəʊk/
Maybe you're right. /meɪbi jɔː ˈraɪt/
You fancy Rick, don't you? /juː fænsi rɪk ˈdəʊnt juː/

Crazes
craze /kreɪz/
frisbee /ˈfrɪzbi/
hula hoop /ˈhuːlə huːp/
inline skates /ˈɪnlaɪn skeɪts/
pogo stick /ˈpəʊgəʊ stɪk/
skateboard /ˈskeɪtbɔːd/
surf clothes /ˈsɜːf kləʊðz/
yoyo /ˈjəʊjəʊ/

Unit 9

9.1 Money
bank /bæŋk/
banknote /ˈbæŋknəʊt/
cash machine /ˈkæʃ məˌʃiːn/
coin /kɔɪn/
credit card /ˈkredɪt kɑːd/
foreign currency /ˌfɒrən ˈkʌrənsi/
gold /gəʊld/
purse /pɜːs/
safe /seɪf/
wallet /ˈwɒlɪt/

9.2 Production and consumption
build /bɪld/
buy /baɪ/
consume /kənˈsjuːm/
design /dɪˈzaɪn/
grow /grəʊ/
make /meɪk/
mine /maɪn/
print /prɪnt/
produce /prəˈdjuːs/
recycle /riːˈsaɪkl/
sell /sel/

9.3 Other nouns
bronze /brɒnz/
corruption /kəˈrʌpʃn/
euro /ˈjʊərəʊ/
fame /feɪm/
forgery /ˈfɔːdʒəri/
fortune /ˈfɔːtjuːn/
hologram /ˈhɒləgræm/
plate /pleɪt/
salt /sɔːlt, sɒlt/
security strip /sɪˈkjʊərəti strɪp/
sheet /ʃiːt/
shell /ʃel/

9.4 Other verbs
assassinate /əˈsæsɪneɪt/
barter /ˈbɑːtə(r)/
copy /ˈkɒpi/
count /kaʊnt/
destroy /dɪˈstrɔɪ/
nominate /ˈnɒmɪneɪt/
rule /ruːl/

9.5 Adjectives
detailed /ˈdiːteɪld/
fine /faɪn/
metal /ˈmetl/
precious /ˈpreʃəs/
rebellious /rɪˈbeljəs/

9.6 Reacting to people
That's interesting. /ðæts ˈɪntrəstɪŋ/
That's a pity. /ðæts ə ˈpɪti/
Fantastic! /fænˈtæstɪk/
Congratulations! /kənˌgrætʃəˈleɪʃnz/

9.7 Linkers
now /naʊ/
then /ðen/
when /wen/

Unit 10

10.1 News topics
culture and entertainment /ˈkʌltʃər ənd entəˈteɪnmənt/
ecology /ɪˈkɒlədʒi/
economics and business /iːkəˈnɒmɪks, ekəˈnɒmɪks ənd ˈbɪznɪs/
health and medicine /helθ ənd ˈmedsn/
lifestyle /ˈlaɪfstaɪl/
politics /ˈpɒlətɪks/
science and technology /ˈsaɪəns ənd tekˈnɒlədʒi/
war and disasters /wɔːr ənd dɪˈzɑːstəz/

10.2 Fame: adjectives and nouns
ambition /æmˈbɪʃn/
ambitious /æmˈbɪʃəs/
fame /feɪm/
famous /ˈfeɪməs/
luck /lʌk/
lucky /ˈlʌki/
popular /ˈpɒpjələ(r)/
popularity /ˌpɒpjəˈlærəti/
skilful /ˈskɪlfl/
skill /skɪl/
success /səkˈses/
successful /səkˈsesfl/
talent /ˈtælənt/
talented /ˈtæləntɪd/

10.3 Other nouns
adhesive tape /ədˈiːsɪv ˈteɪp/
cable car /ˈkeɪbl kɑː(r)/
crocodile /ˈkrɒkədaɪl/
exhaustion /ɪgˈzɔːstʃən/
honeymoon /ˈhʌniːmuːn/
mansion /ˈmænʃn/
marathon /ˈmærəθən/
proposal /prəˈpəʊzəl/
Rolls Royce /ˌrəʊlz ˈrɔɪs/
toothpaste /ˈtuːθpeɪst/

10.4 Other verbs
attach /əˈtætʃ/
celebrate /ˈselɪbreɪt/
explode /ɪkˈspləʊd/
photograph /ˈfəʊtəgrɑːf/
propose /prəˈpəʊz/

10.5 Adjectives
dramatic /drəˈmætɪk/
exclusive /ɪkˈskluːsɪv/
platinum /ˈplætɪnʌm/

World of English 5

Useful expressions
Cheers! /tʃɪəz/
Good to see you. /gʊd tə ˈsiː juː/
It really suits you. /ɪt rɪəli ˈsuːts juː/
Never mind! /ˈnevə maɪnd/

Special days
candles /ˈkændlz/
cards /kɑːdz/
Christmas tree /ˈkrɪsməs triː/
costumes /ˈkɒstjuːmz/
decorations /ˌdekəˈreɪʃnz/
Father's Day /ˈfɑːðəz deɪ/
fireworks /ˈfaɪəwɜːks/
lights /laɪts/
Mother's Day /ˈmʌðəz deɪ/
presents /ˈprezənts/
Saint Valentine's Day /sənt ˈvæləntaɪnz deɪ/
stockings /ˈstɒkɪŋz/
Thanksgiving /ˈθæŋksˈgɪvɪŋ, ˈθæŋksgɪvɪŋ/
turkey /ˈtɜːki/